FACING LIFE'S CHALLENGES

A Psychotherapist's Guide to Inner Healing

Dr. Vera Gallagher
and
Kathleen Stauffer

Sheed & Ward
Kansas City

Names and identifying characteristics of clients mentioned in this book have been changed. In addition, patient confidentiality has been honored in all accounts; no clinical information contained herein has been used without permission of the client involved.

Names of sisters, friends, saints, and their locations are factual.

Sheed & Ward™ is a service of The National Catholic Reporter Publishing Company.

◆

Library of Congress Cataloguing-in-Publication Data

Gallagher, Vera.
    Facing life's challenges : a psychotherapist's guide to inner healing / Vera Gallagher and Kathleen Stauffer.
        p.   cm.
    ISBN: 1-55612-864-9 (alk. paper)
        1. Counseling. 2. Psychotherapy.   I. Stauffer, Kathleen, 1963-   .
II. Title.
BF637.C6G33   1996
158-dc20   96-23926
                                                                CIP

◆

Published by: Sheed & Ward
                115 E. Armour Blvd.
                P.O. Box 419492

Kansas City, MO 64141-6492

To order, call: (800) 333-7373

Contents

The chapter on forgiveness has appeared in St. *Anthony Messenger*. "Prayer: Keep It Simple" and "Working Your Way Back From Tough Times" have appeared in *Our Sunday Visitor* in shortened form. Also, versions of the chapters on stress, pennies for Portland, teenagers, addictions, and anger have run in *Catholic Digest*.

Thanks to Billie Sweeney and Ralph Huskey, co-chairs of the Board of Directors of Shepherd's Counseling Services, and to executive director Judy Barnes for the creativity they devote to Shepherd's fund-raising efforts. Their hard work makes affordable therapy possible for the many women and men who struggle for wholeness, and for peace of spirit.

My appreciation, too, goes out to the many clients who see me for therapy through SCS, and to the thousands of men and women who share their lives with me through letters and phone calls each year. They inspire me more than they can ever know.

I want also to express gratitude to my friends at the United Indians of All Tribes foundation, who have enriched my life with gifts of age-old wisdom, patience, and spirituality.

Many thanks to the Good Shepherd Sisters who love and support me now and have done so for the past 60 years of my happy and rewarding life.

Finally, special appreciation to my co-author, Kathleen Stauffer, from whose expertise I have profited both in her work as managing editor of *Catholic Digest*, and in writing this book.

Dedication

To Cathy, Geralaine, Ed, Rosemary, Diane, Barbara, Rick for reasons they know best.

– Dr. Vera Gallagher

Big thanks to *Catholic Digest* assistant editor Michael McCarthy and to our systems coordinator Heidi Hansen. Their patience with and knowledge of computers far exceeds my own, and I appreciate their good-natured willingness to lend a helping hand. My appreciation also to *CD*'s assistant to the editors Margaret France for those days when she makes my life easier.

But I owe much more to Sister Vera Gallagher, who has so generously allowed me to be her "words" in this book, a project that, because of her extraordinary talent for working with others, will help so very many people.

– Kathleen Stauffer

Preface

Where your treasure is, there is your heart. This book is a treasure. It is a treasure because it reveals the heart of Vera Gallagher over her long and fruitful life as an educator, therapist, and Roman Catholic nun. For almost eighty years, her heart has struggled bravely with damaged people, loved them in their self-contempt, and accumulated a storehouse of anecdotes full of her choicest wisdom. This is a book that is a window into one woman's fierce and tender treasury of love.

In these pages, you can recognize your own story in the many personal encounters Dr. Vera Gallagher discloses. Written from the experience of one who has walked with some of the most broken hearts of our human family, no wound or sadness is too daunting for her to face forthrightly and with faith. Panic, addiction, eating disorders, incest, post traumatic stress – these are only some of the topics treated in this veritable treasure of compassion and sage advice.

Yet the treasure here is not easy booty. It is not fool's gold or glittering tinsel without substance. The treasure in these reflections is full of challenge and paradox. These pages do not invite the reader to skirt life's pain and hardship. The treasure here is found in assessing what is truly valuable and then committing oneself wholeheartedly, embracing self-improvement and then living out that value.

In his recent picaresque novel, *The Alchemist,* the Portuguese writer Paulo Coelho tells how the hero of the story, a shepherd boy, meets a monk in order to learn about true treasure.

The monk tells the shepherd about an old man who lived in Rome at the time of Tiberias Caesar. The old man had two sons – one a soldier, the other a poet. Then the old man has a dream, and in the dream an angel tells the man that the words of one of his sons will be immortal for all ages. The old man's treasure is the pride he feels in his two sons, particularly in the one who writes such spellbinding verse.

Eventually, the old man dies and goes to the gate of heaven, where he is met by the same angel he saw in his dream. The angel asks if the old man has any request before he enters heaven. His only regret, the old man says, is that he has died before finding out how later generations would appreciate the immortal poetry of his genius son. He would like to know what works of his son were particularly esteemed by future peoples.

In the realm of heaven, the angel explains to the old man, it is possible to go forward or backward in time. So the angel takes the man twenty centuries into the future. "Your son the poet, who was all the rage of Rome during the reign of Tiberias," says the angel, "dropped from view after the death of the emperor, and his words have been lost to the obscurities of antiquity.

"Your son the soldier went on to become a centurion in the Roman legions. Though a strong warrior, he was known as well for the care of his own servants. Indeed, when one of his household became sick, he invited an itinerant healer to minister to his servant. When the healer offered to come to his house, your son spoke words of faith that are uttered on human lips all over the world even to this day: 'Lord, I am not worthy for you to come under my roof. Say but the word and my servant shall be healed.'"

This book is a treasure because it will challenge your assumptions about what is really valuable. It will urge you to befriend your own deep pain and hardship. It will take you by the hand and walk with you as you make the choices to live a more free – yet disciplined – life.

This book is a treasure because it reveals the heart of one who has faced her own pain, and painstakingly sought what is of authentic value. Reading this book is like entering a warehouse of precious gifts. You have only to turn its pages and see if your heart does not long for the same treasure Dr. Vera Gallagher has found in her own heart's desire.

Rev. Craig Boly, S.J., Ph.D.
Pastor, St. Joseph Church
Seattle

Introduction

Could This Be You?

You want happiness and peace. Fulfillment. But your ideas and plans don't turn out. You're angry much of the time and don't know why. You've got the talent, you know that.

But you're depressed, sad, lots of angst. Why? Maybe you're like the client who said, "I tried to work it off. I bought a bat and ball, hit that ball all over the back yard until my shoulder ached. Didn't do me any good. I got an axe, and chopped wood until the blade turned dull. No relief there. I snap at my kids for no reason. I must stop. But how?"

You had thought that when you got married, had two nice kids and a spouse who worked hard and was faithful, you would feel better. But now you have two lovely children, a good partner, and you feel terrible: You're only 35, and already you creak and groan with arthritis. There's pain in your joints, knees, ankles, fingers, wrists.

Or maybe you have TMJ (Tempero Mandibular Joint, the result of grinding your teeth due to stress). Your head screams like a sonic boom. Why won't the pain stop?

Or perhaps you've got your Ph.D., a circle of professional friends, attend high-brow meetings. You teach a couple of classes of graduate students. But you're lonesome. Always lonesome, in the middle of a crowd. Why this alienation? You and your spouse are compatible, and you love each other. Why the dread of losing the one you love? What can you do?

Or maybe you never did marry because you were too busy supporting your birth family, yet you ache for parenthood and children.

Or perhaps you're a mother who races to work in the morning, works all day, picks up the kids from school, makes dinner, helps the children with their homework, and then collapses into bed – and the next day is exactly the same. Maybe you're a father who holds two jobs to make money enough for the family but never gets time to watch the little ones grow up. Why do you feel so agitated?

Why are you so terribly overweight? "Big Mama," they call you, or "Big Daddy." You've gone on lots of diets, spent fortunes on them, but the weight always comes back. Why can't you get it off and keep it off? Why do you feel hungry all the time?

How can you stop the closet drinking, the sneaking of mints to cover up the alcohol on your breath? How much longer can you conceal the secret from spouse and family? How can you hide the financial outlay? How can you deal with addiction?

Why can't you forgive childhood injury and pain within your own home? Why do you try and try, but it never really feels like it's over? Christians are supposed to forgive, aren't they? Everybody is supposed to forgive. All the books say so. So why can't you forgive?

Why do you have such low self-esteem? Why do you feel like you ought to take care of everybody else? What makes you want to become invisible? Others tell you that you're a good worker, that you're good-looking. But you can't feel proud of yourself. Not ever. How do you develop self-esteem?

Do Any of the Above Apply? What Unanswered Questions Do You Pack Around? What Can You Do About It?

Each and all of the above illustrations can result from bits and chunks of childhood pain and grief swimming around in your unconscious mind.

No childhood's perfect, after all. Not even Adam and Eve did a really hot job with their kids – or why would one have murdered the other? Our own parents aren't perfect either, though their intentions might have been the best. Like they say, pie in the sky really is pie in the sky, sitting up there in the fluffy clouds, ready to melt with the sunset.

This inspirational book will introduce you to ways and means of recovering wholeness, as well as tell you about dozens of persons who have struggled with the same kind of problems you have and achieved healing. Perhaps, after you have finished reading this, you can look critically at yourself and note a problem or two – we've all got them. Myself, I have a dozen. It's not disloyal to look back and say, "Yeah, that's how it was, not all black, not all white, not all gray – just splotches of black and gray on a white background."

Intelligence and memory are most receptive during childhood. Whatever is learned then is unconsciously re-enacted throughout life. If, for instance, one sibling got more parental attention than you, it's possible that, in adult life, you suspect that others grow greener grass in their own back yards, have all the fun, sail along on the jet stream. You, meanwhile, are stranded, overlooked, forgotten.

It's important to recognize where these feelings started. Once acknowledged and dealt with, negative emotions can die out. Then, instead of feeling inferior, you can work on diverting old energies into celebrating life with new joy.

Healing from bits and pieces of childhood grief can be simple, or it can be complicated. Most adults can discover and work through old habits with a little bit of help – perhaps, even, from a book like this one. Others may need therapeutic guidance. In the old days it was considered a disgrace to see a therapist. In the present, a therapist on the hook is an honor. Whatever solutions may be called for, however, first things must come first: As adults, we need to own the problem. After that, we can find remedies.

Is This Book For You?

This book is for you if you're afraid to take a glance back over your childhood to discover what aspects of child-rearing may have hurt you. Mature adults know and accept that nobody in the world is perfect, neither themselves nor their parents. A recognition of current problems with a backward look to discover their origin can help grown-up children immeasurably. It can also help with an adult's current child-rearing responsibilities.

This book is for you if you currently suffer from debilitating physical symptoms for which your physician can find no physical cause.

This book is for you if you can't stop worrying. Or if emotional problems like frequently losing your temper block your progress in life. Or if your marriage is in trouble because of everyday stress, addictions, and a sense of failure.

This book is for you if you want to enjoy life, the thrill of living today, the joy of blue skies and green grass, the happiness of friendship, the pleasures of good physical health, the satisfaction of a job you like. Most important, this book is for you if you seek fulfillment, the pleasure of becoming fully attuned to the world and all that's in it.

How Do I Know?

For 50 years I have worked with teenagers and adults who have suffered from a variety of problems. For them, I have offered counseling and constructive therapy. And I have published more than a thousand articles and five books besides.

Through it all, I've had the joy of working individually with at least 3,000 disturbed teenagers – and watching them go on to live productive and happy lives. I've listened to, read letters from, talked over the phone with, given workshops to thousands of adults throughout the English-speaking world.

I'm a therapist whose joy it has been to help men and women name their problems, discover those lost bits of childhood, deal with them, and then move forward and win. I've stood by while workers who never got a promotion started rising through the ranks; while persons who thought they could never cope with college have walked off with degrees; while unhappy married partners learned to taste the sweet joys of intimacy and love; while addicted adults traveled into sobriety; while physically unstable persons regained health and life; while desperately lonesome adults found friendship; while dependent grown-up children developed into independent adults; while clients discovered skills and talents they never dreamed of.

Professionally, I work out of the cognitive-behavioral perspective. My techniques reflect a way of looking at human behavior that has led to successful prescriptions for change. Nevertheless, applications that work for one client might not be successful with another. We humans are complicated persons and each one of us is uniquely individual. Therefore a solution suggested in any one chapter might not be effective with a particular reader. Because we are gifted with intelligence, it may be useful for readers to conceptualize how different interventions might be applied in a variety of ways.

My clients inevitably introduce God or a Higher Power into the counseling situation. They may never attend church or belong to a formalized religion, but unfailingly they make spirituality an integral part of the conversation – perhaps at the first session but, more likely, at some mid-point in the journey. Consequently, God's help and gifts form a running thread throughout this book.

I'd like to meet with every individual who could use professional assistance, but that's not possible. So I've written this inspirational book instead. It's about healing, and in this book I'll ask the questions that might help you recognize your old ways of thinking and acting, ways that are no longer productive. For this reason, I've included many true stories of former clients – with their permission, though their names and other identifying details have been changed. All of them have labored with disabilities similar to your own. But each successfully overcame these disabilities, and it's my hope that their stories might spur your own healing journey and give you the hope that will help you succeed. Most of you can make your own journey to wellness through the search and discovery process provided here. Some may need the assistance of therapists – but even then, remember: It's far better to know what one needs than to fruitlessly wander down one-way roads to nowhere.

This book is for you if you want to heal your mind, your body, and your spirit. This book is for you if you want to get the most out of life, live long enough to enjoy your grandchildren, find the career you've secretly longed for, rejoice in good health, and make the world a better place because you've lived in it.

May you enjoy reading this book as much as I have enjoyed watching clients grow into happiness and fulfillment.

Dr. Vera Gallagher
Seattle, Washington
May 1996

ONE

Self-Esteem Power

Sara phoned long-distance the other day. She wanted to chat, but she also had some questions for me. Currently Sara is in one of California's big cities taking care of a man dying of AIDS. In the meantime, she is paying rent on her apartment in Palm Springs. Once, several years ago when she needed help, he reached out to her. Now many of his friends have died of AIDS, and he is alone. So Sara is looking after him because of that kind act long ago.

Sara mentioned that occasionally he did not act like himself. "Do persons with AIDS sometimes suffer dementia?" she asked. I answered that is a possibility before the end.

"When I had a psychotic break once," Sara said, "you took care of me."

That was true. As a teenager Sara had been placed in our Good Shepherd school in a western state. At the time, I was both principal and head of the social work department. During those years, Sara had two psychotic breaks. Each time, I called an ambulance and accompanied her to a psychiatric facility in a distant city. On both occasions, Sara underwent shock treatments.

On her return to the school, Sara had memory problems and strange little mannerisms. She would outgrow them, I knew. But the other teenagers would tease her, so at times I kept Sara in my office if she was not actually scheduled for a class. She was so relieved to be close to some person who cared for her that she'd simply sit there, quietly and happily. Now she was recalling that time.

I had two brief psychotic breaks, Sara was telling me, and you stayed with me. I will stay with my friend.

Sara doesn't realize it, but she is giving her self-esteem a terrific boost. Why? Because thinking for ourselves increases self-esteem. Whenever clients ask, "What shall I do?" I counter with a question of my own: "What do you think you need to do?"

I doubt that God likes wimps. Helplessness achieves neither self-esteem nor the Kingdom of God. Dependence on others can be comfortable, but it cannot be constructive for the ego. Once we've determined a goal, the struggle onward despite obstacles is the road to self-esteem

Further, to assert ourselves in life so we might accomplish our goals is by no means frowned upon by our Creator. Certainly, Jesus was assertive. When the Pharisees complained because Jesus allowed a public sinner to wash his feet in their living room, Jesus answered that *they* had not bothered, in accordance with custom, to wash his feet. Somehow or other, the task needed to be accomplished. And so he defended the woman who got the job done. On another occasion, weary of the endless efforts to trip him up, Jesus called his inquisitors a "brood of vipers." Strong language, but appropriate self-assertiveness is necessary for healthy self-esteem.

Often I am asked: "How can I develop my self-esteem?" Sometimes the question is posed from Anyplace, U.S.A. Occasionally, the question is asked via long-distance calls. Most often, it is asked by clients in my office. Unfortunately, seekers frequently hope for a three-minute recipe; but it's not that simple.

What is self-esteem, anyway? Self-esteem is an innate sense of self-worth that enables us to accept ourselves as essentially good persons capable of dealing with life's challenges, of making a positive difference in the lives of others, and of living in accordance with God's plan.

And the best model of self-esteem available is Jesus. Jesus knew he would live his life for God, for his own self-development, and for others. He was certain that God's blessing was with him. You and I have the same certainty: God made us, God guides us, God loves us, and God expects us to love ourselves and others.

Certain that I'm made in God's image and likeness, I have confidence in my ability to think and to cope with life's challenges, whatever those might be: marrying, raising children, committing to a religious vocation, teaching, doing office work, enduring the mid-life crisis, suffering from sickness and pain, or even surviving success, old age, and death with dignity. I know I'm on a journey to human wholeness and happiness, that I have legitimate needs and wants, that I deserve equal treatment regardless of the color of my skin or my nationality or my religion or my giftedness.

Those might sound like simple, well-known truths, but they form the basis for that genuine self-esteem which is a basic human need. With self-esteem we can face and overcome dangerous or difficult situations; without self-esteem, we crumble before obstacles and pain.

During the time of slavery in this country, the underground freedom train for slaves ended in Windsor, Ontario, as well as in other Canadian locations. Recently I visited the homestead of the first slave who made it to freedom in Windsor. (Actually his dying master *had* given him his freedom, but other slaveholders would not have accepted his free status, so he had to use the underground railroad anyway.) Hearing the story of his courage and daring, I knew that it was self-esteem that had enabled John Freeman Walls to overcome almost insurmountable odds and make his way to freedom.

Self-esteem is needed to cope with today's America, too. These are times of great change, and when we face change, we face choices. Our self-esteem often governs our choices. Persons who think little of themselves are likely to choose acquaintances who belittle them. Again and again I've watched a battered woman leave the batterer and walk into the arms of the next partner who does likewise. Because such a woman has a low or almost nonexistent self-esteem, she gravitates to those persons who treat her as she feels she deserves. In our Los Angeles outreach, in fact, Good Shepherd Sisters who house battered woman and children provide mental health counseling and therapy to raise the women's and children's self-esteem. Further, they ask the women to stay one year so they will leave prepared to look for healthy relationships.

Self-esteem promotes self-confidence and self-respect so we know our abilities and limits. We take up those challenges we can meet and refuse those we cannot. Sometimes I meet clients who try to accomplish the impossible, simply because they cannot say no. They don't respect themselves enough to refuse overwork so supervisors and others use them.

One client was a reliever on a job that called for 10-hour workdays. The pay was good. But she was inevitably summoned on weekends when others wanted time off. Gradually the position grew into a six-day workweek, 10 hours a day, with no free weekends.

She discussed the problem with me, but lacked the self-esteem to say, "I can't do this." Finally the woman broke down, weeping with sheer exhaustion, suffering because she couldn't spend time with her own husband. Of necessity she was forced to face facts and tell her boss she could not continue the pace. The solution turned out to be simple: The boss engaged a second employee so the burden could be shared. To accept ourselves and our limitations promotes self-esteem.

In the Gospels Jesus sought out lonely spots where he could pray. He had no qualms about leaving the multitude and rowing to the other side of the lake where he could be alone, or stealing away to a mountain top. Jesus took care of his human and spiritual needs, and invites us to do the same.

Why is self-esteem essential?

More than any other gift, our minds are precious. But we can't freely use intelligence without self-esteem because we can't dare to think, to create, to explore uncharted areas of human endeavor. We can't learn how to dress or even how to obtain food without using our minds. Without thought we can't make choices, wise choices, those choices on which our own welfare and the welfare of those intimately connected with us depends. Nor can we make those choices that ultimately determine our salvation.

Especially sad to observe are those who dull intelligence with alcohol and drugs. Persons who stumble into this lifestyle may want to escape the pain of freedom, or numb mental pain that hurts too much to bear. Whatever the reason, it's important to recognize that alcohol and drugs are not so much a choice as a free fall into emptiness and despair. In many cases drugs and alcohol were used in the adult-child's home, and were drifted into as an escape route from reality. But pickling the brain does not bring happiness.

How can I develop self-esteem? I hear that question so often.

"Sister," many people say, "I've tried and tried to improve my self-esteem, but I still feel like dirt. What can I do?" I'll suggest some answers.

Home and the environment are important factors in the life of the growing child. The child who is unwanted, victimized by abuse – physical or sexual – neglected by parents who are addicted or overworked, or who is left to grow up with less care than is bestowed on the front lawn will form a negative self-image. Such a child may feel worthless and useless. Those feelings are the seed for serious problems in the teenage and adult years. And such an adult-child may well need professional help to develop self-esteem since parents and home environment are primary factors in initiating self-esteem.

Despite the importance of childhood years in the development of self-esteem, however, self-esteem is acquired, not given. Indeed, the development of appropriate self-esteem and self-confidence is one our biggest life tasks. From the moment we attain adulthood, we accept responsibility for our own growth and character formation.

Moreover, adults can't fashion self-esteem from the approval or approbation of others. Performing excellently, serving everybody for the sake of praise, stifling personal identity to please others – these will not raise our self-esteem. (Eventually, as age catches up, we can't maintain the pace anyhow.) And we won't get self-esteem from personal beauty, lovely clothes, or the acquisition of things. (Beauty doesn't last, clothes go out of style, and possessions can disappear overnight.) A genius I.Q. or literary ability don't bestow self-esteem, either. (A stroke tomorrow might devastate both.)

Self-esteem sprouts from a budding awareness that God made me and loves me, that God is my ultimate goal, and that my aim in life is to observe God's law and consciously live it. Freely directed behavior, and the knowledge that I make choices congruent to my goal of loving God and others is the foundation of self-esteem. Nobody will do this perfectly, but when I make mistakes, to acknowledge them and ask God's forgiveness leads to self-esteem. To be sure, Jesus, who models self-esteem and self-confidence, always maintained a healthy awareness that he came to do God's will.

In addition, evaluating life situations in light of reality is another crucial element in nurturing self-esteem. We can allow ourselves to drift into unreal thinking and actions, but it's costly. One friend, for instance, has not done her income taxes for the past five years, though her income is no more than average. She spends hours and days worrying about those unpaid debts to the government, writing letters, fielding calls from the I.R.S., and setting up days on which to complete the proper forms.

Curious, I asked why she never actually completes the task. "I can't get all the material together," she said, "all those receipts, all those bills."

"Why not?" I countered.

"They're all in different boxes and my house is such a mess I can't find anything."

"Why not engage a cleaning person for one day?"

"I'm ashamed," she explained, "to let anybody see the mess." Unreal thinking.

Meeting and facing obligations in an upfront manner is another way we can boost our self-esteem. When we act in accordance with our values, we increase self-esteem, too. Jenny told me that she felt guilty, for instance, because she habitually took home small items from the office: pens, paper clips, envelopes. The amount of money involved would have amounted to little, but the actions nibbled away at her sense of self. Nobody else knew, but Jenny knew.

Recognizing small dishonesties we might otherwise dismiss because "Everybody does it," and then eliminating the behavior can also raise self-esteem. In other words, observing God's law is essential for self-esteem. Bibles are easily available, and so are courses in Scripture. It's our obligation to discover God's call, and respect it. I have one client in particular whose main concern, day by day, is to keep her actions in harmony with God's commands. Often, she prays for God's guidance.

Jenny's childhood was filled with tragedy. In the past she has even contemplated suicide. Now she is developing into a woman sure of her competence, a woman with an increased sense of self-worth. She is growing into self-esteem.

I'd like to list six quick steps to self-esteem, but I can't because self-esteem is built slowly. There are no quick fixes. But I do know that holding God's hand while we struggle to grow in self-esteem and self-confidence day by day until we become fully alive is one way we can nudge our struggle along.

"The greatest glory of God," one of the Church Fathers wrote, "is a person fully alive."

SUMMARY

Self-esteem does not stem from the approval or approbation of others. And it doesn't spring from the way we look, what we wear, or what we own. Self-esteem is an innate sense of self-worth that enables us to accept ourselves as essentially good persons capable of dealing with life's challenges, making a positive difference in the lives of others, and living in accordance with God's plan.

Highlights

- Jesus is a good model of self-esteem since he knew he was living his life for God, for his own self-development, and for others.
- Having self-esteem means understanding that we're on a journey to human wholeness and happiness.
- A solid sense of self-esteem enables us to expect equal treatment with others.
- Self-esteem is acquired, and developing it takes time.

Discussion

1. How does self-esteem help us cope with life's challenges?
2. What evidence in the New Testament shows that Jesus had healthy self-esteem?
3. What can we do to develop our own self-esteem? Make a list to review from time to time.

TWO

Anxiety Happens

Teresa was 17 when she had her first anxiety attack. She doesn't recall where it occurred, but she will never forget the distress of it: She couldn't get her breath and began gasping for air; her heart started pounding as though it would hammer right through her chest. Perspiration poured out of her body, and she trembled violently. Teresa had to escape someplace where she could regain control of herself – alone. She didn't know what triggered the attack.

But it came again. And again. And again. Each time, her heart accelerated madly, she trembled, and she couldn't breathe. Teresa definitely could not attend school. She was afraid this terrifying problem would resurface in the presence of her peers, who might tease her.

To be sure, most of us feel anxious when we encounter a new situation, take an exam, go out on a first date, meet with a therapist. That is natural.

But some of us are overcome with such paralyzing anxieties that we routinely expend a great deal of energy – energy we need to apply elsewhere in our lives – to cope with the fear. About 5% of the U.S. population suffers from acute anxiety, and around 1% are disabled by it. About 20 to 30% of Americans have suffered from one or more panic attacks. The majority of victims are women, though as a therapist I see men with acute anxiety as well. Also, a recent study in Science News found that anxious middle-aged white males were more likely to develop high blood pressure than anxious white females or older white males. So it might be, then, that men tend to develop high blood pressure while women develop the usual syndromes typical of acute anxiety.

At any rate, I do know that such anxiety is a real problem, and not only because it causes those who suffer from it emotional pain. "Anxiety can make you suffer, but it can't kill you," is a piece of folk wisdom that may not be true. A study reported in the *Journal of the American Medical Association* in October 1991, for example, noted an excess mortality among 3,302 patients who suffered from "pure" anxiety neurosis.

Anxiety attacks often start like Teresa's did, with short spells of symptoms that occur suddenly, without warning, and for no apparent reason. Victims feel they have lost control and dread they will be noticed.

Some feel as though their legs are unable to function properly. Consequently, these people stagger or walk in an unusual fashion. It's as if the ground has shifted and now they fear their feet won't hit it going down. Or, when walking, stricken individuals may suddenly feel their legs turn to jelly, and thus grab onto somebody nearby with a frantic reach.

Such attacks are likely to start in the late teens and early 20s and appear not to be occasioned by any specific factor. Indeed, such attacks differ from the more usual forms of anxiety for which an origin can be found: A person who is fearful of dogs may recall, as a child, having been bitten by a dog; one who is anxious about a coming plane trip may remember that a friend or loved one or an admired celebrity died in a plane crash.

But the true danger with unexplained anxiety attacks is that, if left untreated, acute anxiety attacks can develop into phobias. One attractive young woman who came to me for therapy was unable to purchase things for herself. She had met with me weekly for months wearing the same outfit – and that was a Christmas gift.

Gradually and slowly we worked together to consider the possibility of a dress purchase. After a considerable period of therapy and struggle, this client did go to a store, select an outfit, bring it to the cashier – and promptly was hit with a panic attack.

There at the counter, the young woman, Dawn, found that she couldn't sign a credit card slip or a check. Because we had discussed *what-might-go-wrong* from every angle, however, Dawn asked the cashier to serve somebody else and give her a few minutes. She was then able to compose herself, sign her name, and walk out with a new dress. In fact, Dawn was so pleased with herself that she returned to the store and bought shoes, a purse, and a necklace to match. Her husband, a business executive, was delighted. He had often pleaded with her to accompany him to business functions, but Dawn couldn't because she had no appropriate clothes to wear.

Dawn was able to cope with the phobia and panic attack because, through our work in therapy, she had come to accept that the crippling anxiety wasn't her fault and was a symptom shared by many other Americans. She had learned that she could deal with an attack and work her way out of it. And, having once worked her way through the terror of a panic attack, she felt encouraged enough to confront her fears again, soon. And she succeeded.

When panic attacks are lived through rather than battled, they lose some of their grip and power.

Consider Lucy. Lucy's mother brought her 26-year-old daughter to me because the young woman was five-foot-five and weighed less than 100 pounds. She was hungry and she did want to eat, but Lucy had suffered panic attacks with severe choking sensations for some time, and feared eating anything other than soft foods like ice cream and Jello.

After Lucy had developed confidence in me, we went out together to McDonald's – not formal dining and not obvious – and ordered hamburgers. As we chatted, both of us ate.

Because Lucy enjoyed the conversation and friendship, she forgot her fear of choking and discovered anew how good food tastes. She had taken the first step in overcoming a phobia: She had taken a preliminary step in a non-threatening atmosphere.

Phobias are irrational but overwhelming fears of an action or situation. They may be overcome by slowly and gradually putting oneself into the situation in a relaxed manner.

As for Teresa, her parents had initially taken her to a physician, a general practitioner. The physician prescribed total rest. Bed rest. No books. No radio. She and her parents cooperated fully.

But it was the worst prescription possible: The teenager had no distraction other than to worry about her anxiety and panic attacks. All alone for hours every day, Teresa fortunately made a move in the right direction. She turned to the only Person left: God.

Consequently, she spent hours in prayer. Though this didn't cure her anxiety, Teresa did experience solace in God's great love.

But Teresa got no better. So, after she had endured six weeks of bed rest without improvement, her physician decided nothing really was wrong with Teresa. Teresa, according to her doctor, was just pretending.

Pretending! It's a diagnosis that underscores every anxiety victim's worst fear. And the more Teresa beat herself up for not "snapping out of it," the worse the anxiety got.

Persons with acute anxiety are likely to suffer also from nausea, diarrhea, and chronic headaches. In fact, 86% of patients with anxiety get severe headaches. In my experience, they are unlikely to take aspirin or other pain relievers. For the anxiety fills the already-anxious person with a thousand dreads: What if I get hooked on drugs? What if the effect of the pain reliever wears off? *Then* what will I do?

In Teresa's case, a year went by. A year during which more than one physician stated that Teresa was faking her symptoms. These diagnoses, of course, only exacerbated the anxiety. Another six months staggered by – time in which Teresa was drawn into an ever closer relationship with God. God never accused her of "pretending."

Eighteen months passed. Teresa gritted her teeth and made herself breathe; she clenched her fists and stopped trembling; willed her heart to slow down. The effort, which was fierce, resulted in severe headaches and backaches. But Teresa was functional. And, having learned that the only entity she could trust was God, she joined a religious Order.

Teresa acquired degrees, held important leadership positions and coped well with everyday life. Meantime, headaches, backaches, insomnia – all slowly, slowly took their toll. Teresa was in her 40s when her health broke down.

The good news, though, is that people *need not suffer* like Teresa did. Patients with acute anxiety can be treated. Anxiety problems are now recognized as part of a larger network of mental-physical disorders, ailments that are both psychological and biological. According to the *Diagnostic and Statistical Manual* (DSM), the fourth edition of which appeared in 1994, anxiety disorders include five distinct categories: panic disorder, phobias, obsessive-compulsive disorder, post-traumatic stress syndrome, and generalized anxiety disorder.

Panic disorder describes the anxiety attacks Teresa suffered as an adolescent. The symptoms approximate those of heart problems or respiratory disorders. Thus, some physicians, finding no physical basis for the symptoms, write such patients off as neurotic or hysterical. Typically, patients end up feeling embarrassed and ashamed.

Of all such disorders, the anxiety with which I'm most familiar is the avoidance of public places and situations associated with the panic attack. The name is agoraphobia, and the disorder is crippling.

On one occasion I was asked to lead a therapy group of seven women in Oregon. Five women suffered from agoraphobia, and could not leave their homes unless a "safe" person was with them: husbands or older children. In this case, their husbands drove them to group therapy, and picked them up later. These women were severely disabled – yet they were bright, articulate, and capable as well.

Of all the anxiety disorders, obsessive-compulsive disorders are among the most difficult to treat. With this disorder, victims become stuck in repetitive thoughts, activities, or preoccupations. One client I treated was stuck on cleanliness. She wiped off doorknobs before touching them. She washed her hands until they were red and painfully chapped. She anticipated germs in every direction, and could defeat them only by practicing incredible cleanliness rituals. She knew her behavior was ridiculous and was embarrassed by it – but couldn't stop it.

Post-traumatic stress disorder, or PTSD, is another anxiety disorder with which I frequently work. It's a possible consequence of any severe emotional trauma: rape, car accidents, war, childhood sexual abuse, fire, floods, airplane crash, captivity. With PTSD, symptoms include nightmares and flashbacks – with the latter often being so vivid the person relives the trauma. PTSD can emerge months or years after trauma occurs. Usually I encounter it in adults who experience flashbacks of childhood sexual abuse many years after the event. The desire to forget all over again can lead to drug and alcohol abuse.

Yet another anxiety disorder, called generalized anxiety disorder, characterizes those persons who are sometimes described as born worriers. They worry about everything, are consumed with worry. They constantly feel shaky and on edge. Often, they are depressed, suffer insomnia, get dizzy spells – and are much more of a pain to themselves than to anybody else.

For persons who fall into all of these categories, however, the prognosis is hopeful indeed. As noted, recent medication breakthroughs *can* make all the difference. I qualify this news, though, since many patients are quite hesitant to follow through as prescribed unless they are simultaneously in therapy with a counselor who has won their confidence. Why? Because, of course, such individuals worry about the effects of the medication in this case as well.

Finally, in her 40s, Teresa got medication from a psychiatrist and discovered a psychologist whose therapeutic intervention was successful. In fact, the vast majority of those who suffer from the various anxiety disorders can and do recover to live full and happy lives.

Frequently the proper medication can control any number of anxiety symptoms: gasping for breath, pounding hearts, choking, walking difficulties, and so on. A problem still exists with some primary care physicians, though, who may not recognize symptoms, or may not be aware of the latest medications.

With acute anxieties and phobias, I myself ask clients to see a psychiatrist for medication. But I've discovered that I may need to work with a client for several weeks or months to build enough trust to get the patient to agree to medication – anxious persons are likely to question every suggestion.

Teresa, who saw me after she moved to the Seattle area, is currently free from anxiety. Headaches are gone. She sleeps well. Medication is no longer needed. Yet, because she had suffered severe anxiety attacks for a very long time, ever since she was a teenager, her anxiety did not go away overnight; Teresa saw a professional for several years. In that time, she needed to discover and deal with all of her underlying hidden fears, and develop her self-esteem.

According to the *American Journal of Orthopsychiatry*, January 1993, a difficult childhood family environment and severe childhood sexual or physical abuse may be predictors of anxiety in adult women. There seems also to be some genetic susceptibility. Victims informed of the genetic possibility more easily accept themselves and lighten up on the typical self-blame.

Self-esteem serves an anxiety-buffering function also, according to the 1992 *Journal of Personality and Social Psychology*. Self-esteem is developed by attaining personal success and satisfaction with life. Usually, then, victims of anxiety are encouraged to get more education, find enjoyable work, develop their abilities. One woman – currently a successful engineer – told me her dearest dream had been a career in art. Yet, at one time she was offered an opening in the field and refused it because her self-esteem was too low to accept the opportunity she secretly coveted.

Social relationships, too, can buffer the effects of stress and anxiety. Everyday contact between neighbors and friends, in particular, according to the 1991 *Journal of Personality and Social Psychology*, prove most effective in fighting symptoms.

When anxiety or panic attacks occur, it's important for the victim to reassure him- or herself that these are not his or her fault, and then try to control breathing.

Should you find yourself fighting a panic attack, follow these steps:

- Take slow, deep breaths, and concentrate on them. Count slowly to six while inhaling and then six to zero while exhaling. Repeat this process over and over. Rather than fight anxiety, accept it with the knowledge that attacks are time-limited and will spontaneously stop themselves.

- Instead of using mental processes to tell yourself how bad, stupid, and worthless you are, imagine yourself walking up a hill with a gradual slope. Tell yourself that on the top of the hill you will meet a Wise Person who will say a word you want to hear.

- Now, envision the trees on the hill, the streams running down it; note the rocks and their different colors; gaze up into the lovely blue sky and the cotton-ball clouds. When you get to the top and meet the Wise Person, ask for the word or gift you need, look at it closely, thank the Wise Person, and then begin the journey back down the hill to a lovely green meadow.

- Lie in the meadow and rest for a while.

By this time the panic or anxiety attack will likely be gone.

Gerry suffered a severe anxiety attack only a couple of days before her vacation. She and her husband had planned on a trip together, but changed plans because Gerry feared getting too far away from me at this crucial point. On the heels of this attack, she accused herself of being "dumb, worthless, a failure, no good" – even though she held a good job and enjoyed a happy marriage.

So I asked Gerry to write seven good points about herself, characteristics of which she was certain; then I asked her to have her husband note the seven qualities in Gerry that he most appreciated; and, finally, I had her ask co-workers and friends to mention the seven aspects of her character that they most enjoyed.

Then Gerry brought the completed paper to therapy, and we discussed the characteristics everybody had noted. Gerry agreed that all these traits were assets for her.

I suggested that when and if an anxiety attack occurred within the next week, she read over the paper, or ask her husband to read it aloud for her. It did prove helpful when the next attack hit.

Anxiety, as noted earlier, can also result from a specific trauma experienced early in life. That was certainly true for Sally, who was 15 when her mother asked me to see her. But Sally was physically strong, very angry, and unwilling to cooperate. Her mother and Sally knew that the teen's father had physically abused Sally. Her mother suspected sexual abuse also, but Sally vigorously denied this. The young woman had, meanwhile, already tried drinking, smoking, sneaking out of the house at night, and partying with "friends" as a means of acting out her deep anger.

Sally was keenly interested in martial arts, too, and at this time was becoming very involved in karate. Very bright, she was bored in school, and so was allowed to attend an alternative school.

But Sally, like many teenagers, was unwilling to talk about her life. Above all she said, "If I was sexually abused, I hope I never remember it."

Through this period, Sally's love for karate increased. And, as a result, she quit smoking, drinking, running around. Hours at karate, in the meantime, mounted until she was putting in 40 hours of training a week. After only one year, Sally won a national karate championship and a gold medal. Now, at age 16, she is in her junior year in high school and plans to attend college. She has developed self-confidence and self-esteem.

And at this point Sally is overwhelmed with post-traumatic stress syndrome. She has begun reliving episodes of childhood sexual abuse.

Often, it's when clients have achieved their goals and are relaxed that PTSD intrudes into their lives. Because childhood sexual abuse is severely traumatic, and because children – too

young to cope with either the emotions or physical arousal of sex –
have stuffed it down and out of consciousness, memories will
come back and the trauma will haunt them at some later point
in life, a point when they are better able to cope with the pain.
Most of the clients I see who suffer from PTSD are between 25
and 40. Those who develop enough resilience to cope with the
pain in their teens, like Sally, are few; but they are fortunate.
Having completed therapy, they will be finished with it.

A few final suggestions on coping with anxiety attacks:

- If driving a car, drive off to the side of the road until it's over.

- Keep at hand some work which is interesting and in which you
  can get involved until the attack is over: needlepoint, art, writing, or something similar.

- When the attack hits, stop and let it run its course. Fighting it
  only makes it worse.

- Expect anxiety or panic attacks. Doing so leaves you free to
  adopt coping mechanisms that prevent fear of having them
  from running your life.

- Do whatever is manageable. Perhaps you simply need to walk
  outside until the attack is over.

- Concentrate on breathing. Count, as suggested in the beginning of this chapter, and let the world go by.

- Picture a place of peace and happiness: on a beach, mountain,
  or valley. Instead of counting breaths, you may prefer to quietly
  and gently use the Jesus prayer.

SUMMARY

Anxiety attacks afflict as much as 30% of the population. For
about 5% of these people, short spells of symptoms that occur
suddenly, without warning, and for no apparent reason can signal
the onset of an anxiety disorder. To be sure, the experience is
frightening for the person affected, because an afflicted individual
feels he or she has lost control and fears others might notice.
There are five distinct anxiety disorders; they include: panic disorder, phobias, post-traumatic stress syndrome, and generalized
anxiety disorder.

Highlights

- Anxiety attacks are likely to start in the late teens and early 20s and appear not to be occasioned by any specific factor.
- They differ from ordinary anxieties, which commonly can be traced to a specific incident or life event. A person who fears dogs, for instance, may have been bitten by a dog in childhood, or, at a young age, been close to somebody who was.
- Anxiety disorders affect our day-to-day activities and our lives.
- Rebuilding self-esteem can help us confront our underlying psychological fears and even help us to overcome anxiety disorders.
- When anxiety or panic occurs, it's important for those suffering symptoms to reassure themselves that they are not to blame.

Discussion

1. How do the five anxiety disorders differ from one another?
2. How has anxiety affected your life? Has it kept you from activities you otherwise might have engaged in? Which activities?
3. Do you ever feel as if you're "losing control" in a public setting? What can you do if this happens?
4. Does your self-esteem (or lack of it) play a role in your fears? Why or why not?
5. Write some fear-fighting exercises for yourself, things you might try if a fear of "losing control" hovers over your shoulder.

THREE

Addictions Can Fracture Our Lives

Recently Peggy spent an hour in therapy with me. She and her husband had been heavily addicted to drink and drugs. "I got sick of myself, just sick with disgust," Peggy says, "and I quit drink and drugs. Period."

She actually did, just like that – with the help of Scripture, to which she turned for the first time in her young life. Then, worried lest her husband drink and smoke himself to death, Peggy planned an intervention and got him into treatment. And here's where the real struggle began.

Peggy's current addiction is compulsive overeating. She wages as intensive a war for control of food as does her husband with alcohol. Over time, our physical selves can get programmed to addictions. And addictions, to paraphrase Isaiah, are like "greedy dogs, never satisfied." Whenever Peggy gets stressed out, she wants to eat. Her husband, on the other hand, wants to drink. (Both, however, have now maintained abstinence from alcohol for more than two years.)

Most of us do have addictions of one sort or other but we don't let them get out of control. Frequent overeating, starving, hard boozing, smoking, sex, drugs, gambling, maxing out credit cards, spending money we don't have are habits that won't disappear by controlling them during Advent or Lent – and then splurging at Christmas and Easter and all the birthday parties in between.

Regardless of how an addiction has begun, the longer it lasts the more powerful it grows. Closet overeaters, for example, may tell themselves, "Nobody will ever know I ate this whole cake if I run down to the store and get another just like it." But their bodies will know, their brains will register this knowledge, and the screws of repetitive behavior will tighten.

When I wrote an article on addictions for *Catholic Digest* in June 1994, more than 200 letters and long-distance phone calls from throughout the U.S. and Canada poured in within two months. Each came from somebody seeking help. Consequently, I will provide factual data in this chapter. (Because the majority of letters and phone calls came from persons with eating disorders, I will deal with those in a separate chapter of this book.)

So let's begin, then, at the beginning:

Addictions are expensive. Currently about 13 million Americans are alcoholic. Each year alcohol kills 40,000 Americans. Every year it costs our country more than $80 billion, is implicated in 30% of suicides (and 46% of teen suicides) and is a factor in one of every four hospital admissions. Alcoholics Anonymous and the well-known Minnesota Hazelden Foundation call alcoholism a sickness.

That statement is disputed occasionally. In the course of chemical dependency studies at Seattle University, however, I learned of a genetic factor found in alcoholics: an ability to metabolize liquor too well. The cause? A liver enzyme called alcohol dehydrogenase; further, about 20% of alcoholics suffer from bonafide psychiatric disorders which they may try to medicate with alcohol.

In my experience as a therapist – I'm not a chemical dependency counselor, but have taken addiction studies – some addicts who determine to quit do so without treatment or AA and maintain sobriety for 20 years or more. Some do so without a support group, regardless of cues in their immediate environment.

Alcoholics can quit, of course – and do so all the time. The problem lies in sobriety maintenance. That's why AA members call themselves "recovering alcoholics," and why they meet weekly in small groups: to maintain sobriety. Currently AA has about two million members, world-wide. AA does not claim to be the only method of recovery, nor to meet the needs of every person.

But food and alcohol are not America's only addictions. In respose to my *Catholic Digest* addictions article, I got many letters from those who wanted to quit smoking and couldn't. Could I help? Well, I could tell them they're certainly not alone.

Actually, says Dr. Michael Fiore, director of the Center for Tobacco Research and Intervention at the University of Wisconsin, "Of the 46 million Americans who smoke, an estimated 80% would like to stop and one-third try each year. Two to three percent of them succeed. There's an extraordinarily high rate of relapse among people who want to quit."

Part of the problem is that nicotine hits the brain quickly and has a potent psychological impact. "The cigarette," says Dr. J. Henningfield of the National Institute on Drug Abuse, "is the crack-cocaine of nicotine delivery." Nevertheless, there are nearly 45 million ex-smokers in the U.S. today. Persons can and do quit.

Why do people smoke in the first place? Nicotine not only gives pleasure, it reduces pain. According to Dr. T. Brandon, State University of New York, Binghamton, "People expect that having a cigarette will reduce bad feelings." Also, says Columbia University psychiatrist Dr. A. Glassman, the act of quitting can trigger severe depression. In fact, when several clients of mine attempted both therapy and quitting cigarettes at the same time, I advised them to continue smoking until therapy had brought them more peace than they currently enjoyed. I didn't minimize the health problems of smoking, but I feared the possibility of suicide when these clients struggled to cope with two stressful situations simultaneously.

Genetics probably play some role in smoking, and definitely advertising does. Various studies also show that, in an addicted smoker, attention, memory, and reasoning ability start to decline measurably just four hours after the last cigarette. Consequently, the urge to smoke again becomes insistent. Withdrawal, then, is not a simple matter: Acute withdrawal lasts from four to six weeks.

Treatment with antidepressants has been quite effective in helping some smokers quit. Besides that, those trying to cut out cigarettes might help themselves by avoiding alcohol, drinking less coffee, changing routine to avoid former cues, anticipating ups and downs, considering a lapse serious. The use of nicotine patches may help. (Some of my clients swear by them; others thought they got no help from patches.) Statistically, about 90% of persons who quit smoking do it on their own.

And while food, alcohol, and cigarettes often dull the nagging discomforts of day-to day stress, we can also become addicted to stress itself. Modern life is programmed for stress. To get all the goodies we want, we hold two jobs, or at least one-and-a-half.

Parties have to be fun, so we exert ourselves to be men and women of good cheer. We expect ourselves to look attractive, and so we have to find the right cosmetics or body lotions. If by any chance sufficient stress is lacking, we create it. We don't like stress, we say, but we're used to it – and what we're accustomed to feels better, even if it's painful.

But what, exactly, is stress? In stressful situations the body manufactures adrenaline and other chemicals such as endorphins, which make us feel good, and shoots them through our systems. Then we're excited, ready to race.

Where? Wherever. The result is that, when we try to slow down, to pray, to relax, to meditate, to get in touch with God, our brains don't shut down so readily. Alarmed with the unaccustomed move into inactivity, our brains continue to pump out messages to nerve receptors to get going again. That makes us anxious, nervous, jittery, motivated to do something . . . anything.

And our addiction to stress, if carried to an extreme, can be dangerous. A friend of mine – who had previously spent several years in prison for bank robberies – confided that he and his companions didn't rob banks for the money. "My family was well-off," he told me. "I didn't need the money. It was the excitement I craved, the planning, the action. After my release, my family of origin closed around me and provided a shield of comfort. I could never have gone straight without them. Every time I felt tension, or something went wrong, I wanted to go out and rob a bank."

A woman, clean and sober for 11 years now, was addicted to heroin for many years. And heavy drug users often steal to support their habits. Once she confided that she believed herself to have been more seriously addicted to the excitement and tension of stealing than to getting high on drugs. She sometimes missed the stress of outwitting the police and planning the break-ins, more than she missed the drugs.

Another friend routinely overworks, but also rises at 4 a.m. daily for an hour of running. That physical activity maintains the stress level in his life, and yet provides relaxation. We Americans are geniuses at inventing ways to maintain high stress levels. Each of us, individually, manages to live a stressed life to some extent. The real danger, though, lies in addiction.

To overcome our addictions – whether to stress, food, drink, or illegal drugs – we *must* pray. We need to slow down, get quiet, grow calm. Yet, programming time for prayer amid all of our rushing around can be extremely difficult. It calls for us to relinquish control of our dash for success, to feel the pain-filled after-effects of the habitual rat race, to endure the discomfort of doing nothing, nothing at all, to ignore the brain's mandate to get up and chase about rather than sit or kneel quietly and open ourselves to God's voice. It can be painful to pray, to listen for that voice which, Isaiah tells us, speaks in a whisper.

But God's time for us is now, this hour, this day, this place. The expectation that in the future – in a different life space, when children are grown, when I get a better job, when I develop self-confidence – I will no longer experience problems with current bad habits is false. God calls us to begin today . . . and to start over again tomorrow, if need be.

"How did prayer help you toward sobriety?" I asked Leona, formerly a heavy heroin addict. The tears came. "I wouldn't be alive," she said, "without prayer." Then Leona poured out God's answers to the prayers of an addict, enough for a book. I'll repeat only one.

Leona passed through two treatment centers. While in each, she managed to get drugs smuggled in; eventually, she walked out of each place. Now she was in a different kind of program for addicts: Its purpose was primarily to help persons in recovery stay out of jail.

In pursuit of this end, Leona got a job. She could not sneak drugs into this place, though, and as a result was doing poorly. "I don't think you're going to make it," her sponsor said. "Is there anything at all that you would enjoy?" Two things, Leona said. One of them was music – if only she had her flute. And roller skates.

"Where is your flute?" the sponsor asked. Leona had left it at her parents' home.

"Write for it," she was told. But Leona couldn't.

"I had just jumped bail," she told me, "and I'd burned my parents for the $8,000 they'd put up. I couldn't ask for anything more."

"Then," her sponsor said, "ask God."

Leona believed in God, but wasn't certain of God. She was trying to work a 12-step program, it was true. But she had hit the bottom of the bottom. "And so I begged God for my music and flute.

"Three days later the music books and flute came in the mail in a package addressed by my mother. No note. Just my music.

"My mother never writes letters and never mails packages," Leona says now. "I don't know of any other time in her life that she mailed a package. But I had prayed, and God got the message across."

One recovering alcoholic described recovery as the ability to see one's life as a story. Prior to recovery, he said, addicts are basically storyless people – too confused to own a coherent story. Moreover, addicts usually isolate themselves, and stories are communal. Stories need a "we." The Bible is a collection of stories which, taken together, tell us about our human relationship with a divine God. AA meetings are places where individuals tell their stories to others, in safety. As AA members put all the individual stories together, they see the mystery of God. Hitting bottom, dreadful as it is, offers one the opportunity of finding God.

Neither brain nor body will ever forget our addictions. The addictive craving will never die. Always, addictions lie in wait, planning to catch us when we are least aware. When we rejoice at Christmas, or at a wedding, or at a party, when there are lots of people around, when it's a wonderful time: that's the moment for the addiction to insert itself greedily into our affairs again.

We can win the addictions war, though, by developing a dependence and trust in God that we can then maintain with regular prayer. Something has got to give; either the merry-go-round, or time spent alone with God. Strangely enough, we find God not by accomplishing, chasing, running. We find God by *not doing*. By surrendering. By just standing still long enough to wait. God created us for love – to love our Creator over all, and to love others as much as we love ourselves.

My client, Peggy, is a particularly good example of how prayer can help us get off the addictions merry-go-round. Peggy dropped one of several jobs to create a space for prayer. Now, her time with God is spent reading a Bible in her home, taking time to think. God has become Peggy's priority, though she was not raised in any religion and never attended any church. She walked a lonely path, but Peggy still found God. The basic longing for God's grace is, I believe, implanted deep within the hearts of every one of us.

"Now," Peggy says, "life is purposeful and clear. I'm setting goals. As of today I've been clean and sober for more than three years, and I haven't touched sugar for more than two years.

"Maybe it's my guardian angel," Peggy adds, "or perhaps the Holy Spirit leads me. I call that small whisper my Guide, and I can tune into it any time. But I try always to keep in touch."

Peggy joined Overeaters Anonymous because of the God-emphasis of the 12-step program that group employs. As she talked to me, Peggy described her homecoming to God. She had known, I think, that the battle against addiction would be painful. In fact, she still misses the food. But her journey to God is authentic, and currently her eyes are fixed on God in the here and now: at this hour, on this day, and in this place.

"I always believed in God," Peggy says. "I just never *talked* to God before."

Peggy could be any of us.

Now she prepares for such occasions as holidays in full knowledge of the challenges they pose. Last Thanksgiving, for instance, Peggy made a list of exactly what she would eat at the family celebration. The Big Dinner was enjoyed that night, but Peggy stuck to foods on her list. "Writing it all down before I smelled the food was important," she explains.

Peggy faces a lifelong battle. God may demand more relinquishments than she has already made. Still, with each victory she grows in freedom. We may not always welcome freedom, however, when we've grown used to our chains.

As food or drink or stress relax their grip on us, we feel an emptiness. We can fill that empty space with God.

In a few months Peggy will no longer be in therapy. I trust her to find, within herself, resources to continue the onward march along her chosen route: Peggy has discovered her own path to God.

Many of us struggle against addictions. Perhaps we feel we're losing the war. No matter. One man I know passed through 50 treatment centers before he gained a sobriety which he has maintained for several years now. Several others have hit 40 treatment centers. What courage! Failures only force us to acknowledge our dependence on God.

One client told me of draining antifreeze out of his car to drink for the alcohol content when he had absolutely nothing else. A woman described sharing needles with anybody, regardless of the risks posed by AIDS or hepatitis, when the need for a shot of dope was urgent. A priest told of directing people to God and prayer when they came to him with serious difficulties in their lives. But God didn't work fast enough. So he, the priest, took all the burdens of those who sought spiritual counsel from him onto his own shoulders. He played God and resolved all problems until he got burned out, exhausted . . . and alcoholic.

The time to begin the struggle against addictions is now. Right now. This day. This year. This moment will not come again. Grab it.

SUMMARY

Addictions cost our society a great deal – not just in dollars and cents, but in human potential as well. And most of us do have addictions of one sort or another. Usually, though, we don't let them get out of control. But the longer addictions do go unchecked, the more powerful they grow.

Highlights

- Neither our brains nor our bodies ever forget our addictions.
- Food, alcohol, nicotine, and even stress can be addictive.
- Understanding that God's time for us is here and now can help us stop numbing out, can help us to live more fully in the present.
- Without some sort of spiritual base, such as God and prayer, we cannot keep addictions at bay.

Discussion

1. How do addictions hurt us?
2. How do our addictions hurt others?
3. What strategies have others used to successfully battle addictions?
4. What strategies can help us fight our own addictions?

FOUR

After Addiction:
Intervention

Frequently I get letters that say, "*My husband . . .* or *my son . . .* or *my daughter . . . is an alcoholic.* Sister, will you please write to this dear relative and explain how serious addiction is, and help my loved one quit? Just don't say I asked you."

I don't write those letters because they would be useless. The *only* person who can help this alcoholic is the alcoholic him- or herself and, under certain circumstances, the concerned and loving person who writes to me. And that person, the person who loves an addict, usually does not know what to do.

Close relatives of an alcoholic or drug addict cannot stop addiction with loving concern, or with advice, nagging, fighting, or spending time on why it happened or endlessly searching for a single, magic remedy.

The only possible solution comes by way of focusing in the here and now: Taking the practical step called intervention.

Addiction powerfully affects the family system. Family members watch their loved one messing up health, life, and the family's economic base. And while a family's love, concern, and courage may undoubtedly be strong, it may, in time, begin to lie dormant beneath layers of frustration and helplessness. If you've tried everything to help and what you've tried just hasn't worked, and if doing nothing is intolerable or may lead to your endangerment, it may be time to try something different: intervention.

Change begins with persons who try to effect change. If the concerned one's help is refused, and if offers of love are rejected, then the caring one needs to direct attention to self and family. Often the caring one and family members have covered up for the alcoholic by pretending, fixing, and controlling persons and situations until the entire family is worn out physically, emotionally, and mentally. Frequently help is next sought from clergy and physicians. But if these persons are not experienced with addictions, then the family may be left with dashed hopes and unanswered questions. When this happens, taking care of the family becomes more important than ever.

Family life with an addicted person is like becoming a hostage. To survive, family members develop varied behaviors, responses, and defenses, which, in themselves, have distinct patterns – or pathologies. The current descriptive word is *codependency* – but many have heard the word bandied about in such a variety of ways that they are weary of it, so I'll avoid the term. Suffice it to say that one who lives in a family with a chemically addicted person is not smart enough, rich enough, wise enough, prayerful enough to escape the trauma or avoid the unhealthy consequences.

Coping with unexpected, unpredictable, and uncivilized behavior consumes so much time, energy, and concern that family members don't have any time left for themselves. Blaming themselves, and hiding the ongoing disruptive behavior, chips away at each family member's self-esteem. And because they live in a crazy world, family members come eventually to no longer expect honest answers, respect, cooperation, and love from the addicted individuals or even from one another. But the real craziness is that family members themselves now feel worthless, guilty, helpless, and hopeless. So they turn to somebody like me, a Catholic nun, or a priest, and say: "You fix it! – we can't."

But they may be mistaken. In most cases, they *can* fix it – with the right kind of professional help.

The technique is called concerned intervention. I have known it to succeed with hundreds of so-called "hopeless" drug and alcohol addicts. Time after time, in fact, I have guided clients through this process, put them in touch with professional chemical dependency counselors, helped provide the support they needed, and shared their success with joy.

Those who have successfully changed the alcoholic syndrome follow six rules:

1. Obtain accurate information.

2. Meet with a professional mental health counselor and with a chemical dependency counselor.

3. Find a support group through group therapy, a 12-step program, or some other reputable group.

4. Learn how to conduct an intervention.

5. Bring the entire family into professional therapy, or a 12-step program such as Alanon, Alateen, or Adult Children of Alcoholics

6. Follow through after treatment. The recovering alcoholic needs continued support andunderstanding.

With her permission, I will repeat the story of one young woman, married to a man she dearly loved who was drinking himself to death. One day in total desperation, she decided she *had* to do something.

The Jo who first started counseling with me was overweight, depressed, and drowning in the murky sea of unworthiness. Thus, the first goal of therapy, for Jo, was getting help to recognize her own self as worthwhile, adequate, and good.

Jo did not immediately tell me that both she and her husband were drug and alcohol addicts, that they camped out on weekends and holidays with drugs and drink. As usually happens, she had seen alcohol abused in her family of origin, and then went on to abuse it herself. Jo spoke, from the beginning, of her deep love for her husband. Then one day she told me she was sick of swilling drink and drugs. She could not develop any sense of self because of her addictions, and so she had determined to quit. And she did. Just like that. No treatment center, no AA. Jo just quit.

The first step for any person who wants to help a loved one escape from chemical addictions, is for that person to quit first. Most persons need a treatment center or group support if alcohol intake has been heavy. (However, some persons do quit alcohol and drugs with no further assistance.) Jo started group therapy at our center, Shepherd's Counseling Services. Though we do not treat chemical dependency, we do deal with problems such as low self-esteem, self-defeating behavior, shame, and depression; all those problems, among others, characterized Jo.

The second step is to find group support. It's not easy to reach outside oneself when self-worth has been bruised and chopped into pieces. But it is necessary. How to find a group? Look in the Yellow Pages for Alanon, Alateen, or Adult Children of Alcoholics (ACOA); meeting with these groups can save the sanity of the partner or child of a chemically addicted person. By listening to others talk, one discovers that the kinds of disruptive behavior one has experienced are known to many others, often with uncanny similarities. When this happens, it gets easier to talk about one's own experience. And that's when healing begins: when one discovers that one is not alone.

Jo, meantime, began recognizing and naming frustrations: Her husband never wanted to go anywhere or do anything. He had only one want: alcohol. Both had planned to spend their vacation time together, but Jo watched her husband give up his vacation day by day because he was too hungover. He'd bought a boat, and Jo had anticipated enjoying time together on the lake, boating. But the boat needed repairs, and Jack had had no energy to work on the boat either.

And Jo was agonizing over more than loneliness: She was worried about her weight, too. Maybe she didn't look good enough to her husband. Their sex life was practically nonexistent. Increasingly anxious about her inability to lose pounds, Jo joined Overeaters Anonymous. And that decision proved to be one of the smartest of her young life.

As Jo took control of her own life, her husband's contrasting behavior became more noticeable to Jo. She was, she realized, terrified that he was killing himself with booze. So Jo persuaded her husband to see his physician for a routine physical. As it turned out, Jo was right.

While Jo's husband was still with the doctor, the nurse asked Jo to step out for a separate consultation. Then the nurse informed Jo that she needed to know several facts: If her husband continued drinking and smoking so heavily, he had only five years to live, at most. The nurse advised Jo to ensure that all bank accounts were joint, that her husband had a will, that money was set aside to cover funeral expenses. Jo walked out in a daze. At her next meeting with me she wept: "What can I do? I love him. I can't imagine life without him."

I advised intervention, described it, and recommended that Jo get in touch with a professional chemical dependency counselor.

The rest of the story is Jo's, and I'll let her tell it.

Intervention According to Jo

My husband had high blood pressure, gout, and was processing alcohol through his skin. That was embarrassing. I realized he was no longer hiding his alcoholism; if I could smell it, so could others. I obtained professional books, read them, and discovered I had failed to recognize the signs of alcoholism. I had lived with an alcoholic for 15 years, but had never admitted it. I always thought an alcoholic was that bum on the corner, or that guy weaving on the pavement. Once I recognized that Jack really was an alcoholic, and suffering from depression, I got scared. He wasn't talking suicide, but I could sense he was that desperate. I read every book I could get my hands on concerning alcoholism prevention. My guts told me that he was, in a hidden way, reaching out. So I believed that intervention would work.

One book talked about reversal. It suggested I reflect on an unacceptable behavior or action, tell my loved alcoholic about it, and state how concerned I felt. It was difficult to pin Jack down because he'd do hit and runs. He'd act, leave, turn away, change the subject, then get angry and defensive. As I continued to point out unacceptable behaviors, over the weeks he stopped those actions. I learned gradually not to accept the consequences of his drinking: I would not call in sick for him, would not buy him beer, would not enable his drinking. I was learning as I went along, and it was tough. I'd take three steps forward, and then three steps back. Simultaneously I prepared financially for an intervention, drew the bottom line, ensured that I would be appropriately cared for whether or not he stopped drinking.

And I continued my research. I attended a free intervention class at a local hospital. I called the health line at my husband's place of employment to discover what insurance coverage we could expect, what kind of support employers would provide. I read books on intervention to learn about the kind of letters we would write.

The letters were extremely important. They were a loving and kind way of telling Jack how I felt, what I wanted him to do, and what would happen if he did or didn't agree – I would leave him. Next, I had to discover who loved him enough to join me in the intervention. Right off I realized he had no friends because he had isolated himself. His adult children do not live in this state. My family refused to participate because they feared his anger. Finally I got lucky: My sister and cousin agreed to join my team. And my therapy group's support was so strong that I dared visit a recovery clinic, meet with a therapist there, and obtain help for myself from staff. Most important, I reached out, told people how awful my life had become, what I lived with, how sick my husband was, how I had hidden it – only to discover, of course, that everybody already knew. I had only *thought* I was hiding Jack's alcoholism.

We rehearsed the actual intervention with the counselor. He play-acted my husband. We decided the order in which we would read our letters, arranged that Jack would go straight from intervention into treatment, and that – if he rejected treatment – I would drive home, pack, and leave.

According to the books I read, before the date of intervention one person must confront the alcoholic, state the problem, ask him or her to get help, and discover how he or she honestly feels. I did this twice, more than a month before intervention. At the first attempt I explained that alcohol smelled off Jack's skin, and I was concerned. Naturally, he was embarrassed and angry. The second time I again told him about the same problem, and asked him to get help. It was on our wedding anniversary. He got very angry, said he had planned on a big drunk and party. "What makes you think I'm an alcoholic?" he asked. Not having anticipated that question, I was stuck. Before I approached him again, I would prepare.

Always, though, I kept the goal in front of me: Life could be good for us.

"How will you get him to the intervention?" asked the members of my group. "I'll say our life together is so bad I want to meet with a marriage counselor, and invite him to come. I'll make it his choice." Personally, I knew he'd come. I knew too that his intention would be to sit there and listen only. But that was all I needed.

The hour and the day arrived. Jack was nervous, I was calm. He chain-smoked. Had I seen the counselor before? he asked. I replied, yes, once. My team was waiting, the counselor introduced himself, and then led us into the back room. Jack was most surprised to see my cousin and sister. Then we sat down and started reading the letters: 13 of them. The letters were written by his family, my family, his kids, his brother. Each letter was

loving, concerned, described the harm alcohol was doing to Jack
as seen by that individual, and asked that he get help.

"What do you want me to do?" Jack responded.

"We want you to go into treatment," the counselor said. Jack
asked if he could do that tomorrow. All of us responded: "No."

Then, he got scared. Jack said he had to wash his clothes
first. Well, we were ready. The books say they will think of the
silliest things. And so we burst out laughing.

He signed some papers, we got directions, and I drove him
home to pack. That was a mistake: I should have had the bag
packed and with us.

At home he grabbed a beer, two beers. "I'm going, " he said.
"This is my last Hurrah!" I was shocked. But he did pack, and we
set out.

Of course, he wanted the most roundabout roads to the
recovery center, and I drove them. We stopped for lunch on the
way. He reached for every delay tactic. Finally, though, we arrived
at the recovery center, and I kissed him goodbye. I was flooded
with tears, guilt, and shock – but all had gone as I begged God
it would.

First, I had prayed God to give Jack insight to realize we
intervened because we love him. Second, I asked that we might
be given time to complete the intervention before Jack got in
touch with his anger.

Never in my most desperate prayers had I dreamed the
intervention would go so well. God was in that room with us.

God was present when I checked Jack into treatment, too.
From his room I could see a chapel and a cross. That's when I
was able to let go and trust God.

But with Jack in treatment, I didn't know what to do with
myself. I couldn't think of where to go, what to do, who would
help. My group therapy was scheduled at 6 p.m. that night. But
what would I do in between? The intervening period should have
been planned. I ended up going to a nearby waterfront and stared
at the water, which calmed me a bit.

Later that day, my group supported me. When I reached
home, the phone danced with lights: The members of my team
as well as my friends wanted to know how I was doing.

How can I describe the changes within myself since intervention? Fears have evaporated. Because I talked out the pain of
living with an alcoholic, I no longer stuff feelings. I'm so happy

Jack is alive and recovering his health. I'm not a Catholic, but the first person I talked to about my troubles and Jack's drinking was a priest, Father Pat O'Neill. He referred me to Shepherd's Counseling Services. I can never thank him enough.

I tell my story in the hope that more persons who love alcoholics will conduct interventions. I want to tell all who live with alcoholics: Don't give up. No matter how bad it gets. No matter how terrible things are. If you are willing to change, you can effect change.

For myself, it's just one day at a time. I don't have to live this way for the rest of my life, only for today. When I began the 12-step program to get my weight under control – yes, I've lost more than 40 pounds – I could do it for only one moment, only 10 minutes, only one hour. But each hour built on the next. Without faith in God, I couldn't have made it, couldn't make it even now.

I was too beaten up from childhood abuse to conduct an intervention. Until God broke through and put a therapist in my life, a support group, a book, I could not have changed my life. Formerly I did not believe that God was interested in me. Certainly, I couldn't imagine that God loved me. But God lifted me up, and I had only to say, "OK, Lord, I see. . . . OK, Lord, I want it. . . . OK, Lord, I can do it because you are with me." Once I knew God, I kept close. Never since have I walked alone.

If, like Jo, you've determined with the help of a professional to conduct an intervention and now you need to write a letter, make sure your letter expresses:

1. Concern. State personal love for the chemically addicted person.

2. Incident. Describe in detail a specific incident in which the C.A. person did something under the influence which was painful, embarrassing, illegal, or contrary to his own value system. Provide dates and details.

3. Evidence. Establish conclusively that drink or drugs were involved.

4. Feelings. Explain how the letter-writer felt at seeing the C.A. person behave under the influence: sad, depressed, ashamed, embarrassed, unhappy, unloved.

5. Concern. Close with a statement of love and care.

But first, engage a professionally trained intervention counselor. Never, never conduct an intervention without professional assistance.

Most insurances do pay for chemical addiction treatment. To involve the employer is important. The strongest motivation for rejecting treatment is often fear of loss of employment. The fact that the employer knows and will pay for treatment is a strong inducement to accept. In fact, according to the *Personnel Journal,* June 1991, "Statistics indicate that up to 90% to 94% of employees offered intervention by personnel managers accept treatment, 97 percent stay in treatment, and 70 percent remain substance-free. . . . However, less than 25 percent of personnel managers implement intervention programs because the process is time-consuming and uncomfortable."

Foresee and deal with every possibility before the meeting: Cover all the what-ifs. Walk through a rehearsal beforehand.

The person who has inaugurated the intervention, moreover, needs to provide a means of support for him- or herself during the hours after the addicted person has checked into treatment.

Certainly, in the case of Jo's family, the prognosis looks promising. Jack has maintained sobriety for more than two years now. His health is markedly improved. Better yet, Jack and Jo's marriage grows stronger, more stable, and more fulfilling year by year.

SUMMARY

Close relatives of addicts cannot stop addictions with advice, nagging, fighting, or endless searching for magic remedies. The only possible solution is intervention.

Highlights
- Successful interventions must be well-planned.
- Successful interventions require the assistance of skilled and experienced intervention experts.
- Living with addicted persons is like being held hostage – we cannot escape on our own.

Discussion

1. What two steps must anyone wanting to help an addicted loved one take before movingforward with intervention?
2. What is "concerned intervention"?
3. How can writing letters help us as well as those we love?
4. What are the five necessary elements of intervention letters?
5. How can rehearsals be helpful?

FIVE

Anger: How Do You Handle It?

Rita complained often that her parents took too much of her time, time she and her husband needed together. "There are endless phone calls," she told me. "They keep coming to visit. We have to go to their place for Thanksgiving and Christmas, when Joe and I want to celebrate together." Over and over I urged Rita to discuss the matter with her parents. Consistently she agreed she would, and just as consistently she failed.

Finally, Rita made a huge determination to talk to her mother. She phoned her, and asked if she might visit to discuss a problem between the two of them. The day and hour were set, and Rita went to her mother's. All day she waited for the perfect opportunity to bring up her problem, but couldn't find an opening. That night Rita had an important meeting but she canceled it. She had promised herself that this time, at long last, she would talk to her mother. She would not leave her parents' house until the act was accomplished.

Rita stayed overnight. All day the next day she watched for an opening and couldn't find one. Finally, as she and her mother straightened up the living room that night, her mother spoke.

"Rita," she said, "you wanted to talk to me about something?"

The time was late and Rita's tongue tripped over itself as she struggled to find the words. Then Rita heard herself explaining to her mother that she loved her, but wanted and needed more time with her own family. She pointed out that, of the adult children, she was the only one expected to stay with her folks all day long at Christmas. She told her mother that her parents phoned too often, asking that she come over and fix this or that. Her mother quietly listened.

Gently, Rita's mother explained that she invited all her children to come at Christmas and Thanksgiving, and that the others left when they wanted. Since Rita and her husband always stayed, her parents figured that was their desire. Rita's mother further explained that she not only invited all her children equally, but she visited them equally, too. Those who were busy at any given time said so, and the parents went elsewhere. She told Rita that nothing was a command performance.

Rita wept with relief. And, as she thought it over, she realized that her mother was right. The other adult children did not visit as often. To Rita, an invitation was a parental command and she had responded as a child, not as the adult woman her parents believed her to be.

And so Rita sat, amazed, in my office. "I was blaming my parents when, all the time," she repeated, "it was my problem."

When God created the first man and woman, I always tell my clients, God made them and succeeding generations good. As Scripture tells us, God looked at this handiwork and saw that it was good.

As a part of that handiwork, God gifted our ancestors with emotions. Among the most powerful emotions is anger. It is also the one many of us find most difficult to deal with. Perhaps because uncontrolled anger is dangerous, many persons learn to keep a tight control over anger – not even admitting the existence of it within themselves. But God made each one of us good, and gifted us with good emotions. Thus, anger is a good emotion, and this becomes evident as we learn to express our anger in accordance with reason.

Occasionally, throughout Scripture, even God becomes angry. Certainly some of the prophets felt angry, and said so. Jeremiah was loud in his complaints to God: "O Lord, Thou hast deceived me, and I was deceived; Thou art stronger than I, and Thou hast prevailed. I have become a laughingstock all the day; everyone mocks me" (Jer. 20:7).

As a therapist, I frequently encounter psychological trauma which is nothing more than a byproduct of anger that has gone unspoken and misunderstood far too long. Unlike Jeremiah, too many of us have not learned to responsibly express anger . . . and then let it go.

Jim has a problem with anger, too. Jim is an artist, but a very unusual artist. Each project he begins ends in failure. Jim can't understand why.

In my work with Jim, I have observed that he makes every attempt at success a disaster. The techniques he uses, in fact, have become quite contrived, even sophisticated. But Jim is totally ignorant of these maneuvers, blind to them. He believes, simply, that he has been preordained to fail. His childhood was normal, he said; college was good; yes, he is talented – and his life is a mess.

Jim certainly didn't come to me asking for help in dealing with his anger. Jim asked for therapy to overcome painful depression. And while therapy has not yet helped Jim to gain the insight he requires, he is, finally, on the right road. His primary problem is that he harbors anger of which he has no awareness. Consequently, he is bewildered by his failures.

Jim's college degree is in communications, but Jim has made no attempt to find work in his chosen field. "I don't know how," he told me. Yet he works in a medical firm as a technical secretary, is well paid – and hates every second of it. "You got work in a medical office though you have no background in medicine," I pointed out. "Why then couldn't you get into the field for which you have been prepared?"

At such questions, Jim could only shake his head in frustration. Then one day, in an unguarded moment, words slipped out from Jim, words he had never planned to utter: "I'm so angry at my parents," he said, "that I don't want to give them the satisfaction of feeling joy over my success."

His own words surprised Jim. He could give no reason for them. He certainly couldn't discuss anger that he knew nothing about, he pointed out. And yet, I couldn't help but wonder if Jim, like Rita, needed only to sit with his parents – as an adult – and discuss his frustrations with them. Quite possibly, they would be as eager to mend fences as he. Right now, however, Jim is merely a gifted person who has effectively hogtied himself.

Both Rose and Jim, in fact, have a couple of things in common. Rose is a talented musician with a trained voice. Yet, except for singing in a church choir, Rose allows herself to use none of her musical gifts.

When Rose attended college, with a major in music, her mother, who belongs to a fundamentalist religion, scolded her over and over for using God's gifts for her own personal advancement. (On the contrary, as Scripture points out in the Story of the Talents, we are *expected* to express our thanks and to glorify God by using our talents.) But Rose did not know how to respond to her mother.

So now she punishes herself (acquiescing in her mother's condemnation), and has done so for years. After the requisite piano recital for her degree, Rose never touched a piano again.

After considerable time in therapy, however, after confronting the anger she legitimately feels, Rose has finally allowed her husband to purchase a piano. I expect the time will come when she will use it again.

The above are only a few examples of the devastating results of unacknowledged anger turned inward. No parent, of course, ever manages to raise a child without making mistakes. In my own practice, I often see patients broken by the extremes of abuse.

But even in better circumstances many of us fool ourselves as Rita and Jim and Rose did. My advice? We must communicate with one another. Not all the anger we feel is necessary. But all the anger we feel must be expressed, discussed, and explored. A healthy parent lets a child express anger, indeed, teaches his or her children how to handle anger appropriately: by talking about it, negotiating, and learning to forgive.

The subject of anger is not one we can afford to skirt in our families. No matter how healthy we are, avoidance is never a good policy. The stories abound. I hear them over and over. Details change but results are the same.

Persons who are angry with just cause need to own and accept that anger. Granted, anger is often an unpleasant emotion which we'd rather not feel or talk about. But unspoken anger, swallowed down and buttoned up, can ruin lives.

A parent or sibling or spouse may deny the long-ago injustice inflicted on him or her, but unless the problem is faced, or at least acknowledged, the effects will be lifelong and crippling. Only when the sore has been lanced can it be exposed to the healing power of God's love. And the lancing must happen.

The reasons for anger, when honestly confronted and discussed, can melt in the light of mutual understanding. But sometimes anger gets drowned in drugs and alcohol, little by little, until the angry person becomes an addict with problems so serious that the primary cause is long forgotten. A significant percentage of the women and men who come to Shepherd's Counseling Services where I practice are in recovery from drug addictions, including alcohol, and must deal now with their original angers or face the probability of relapse.

I encourage clients who cannot, at this point, talk out their angers with the person(s) responsible to express their feelings on paper: write or draw their angers. Some use color to help express anger, some create objects like a cookie monster or a play-dough villain. A few scribble their feelings into poetry. Once objectified, angers are observed more clearly and become more difficult to ignore.

Some preliminary rules:

1. Because home computers are common and faster than writing by hand, some clients prefer to work by computer. In that case, make certain that nobody else has access to the writing. One woman, who was angry primarily at her husband, left her computer disks handy when she left for a few days vacation. Her husband found and read every one of them. The fight when she got back was more bitter than any that had preceded it.

2. Do not share writing or drawing immediately with anyone except a therapist. Wait a day or two. When you read it over later, you may decide that nobody else should see the raw emotion. Also, a couple of days later you may have learned how to make your statements more concrete and powerful.

3. The same goes for a letter. Never mail an angry letter the day you write it. Wait a couple of days. When you read it over then, you may decide not to send it. Very confrontational material is likely to draw an equally aggressive response. One client, for instance, in moments of rage made posters from a photo of her mother, wrote "child-abuser" underneath, and stuffed them in the neighbors' mailboxes. Needless to add, she was hauled into court for a federal offense. "Why didn't you ask me?" I queried. She grimaced ruefully, "Because I knew you'd say 'Don't'."

4. Periodically look through, read, absorb all you've written, painted, or created. This provides an opportunity to realize the progress you've made, and that discovery is empowering.

5. When in the grip of strong emotion – anger, anxiety, depression – take a walk. Even a 10-minute walk helps. "I don't have the energy," you say. But a brisk short walk is energizing. Besides, depressed persons who don't have energy enough for a quick walk are likely to have sufficient energy to make it to the

refrigerator, find something sweet, and swallow it down. No energy?

6. Create a circle of friends, a substitute family, within which it's safe to vent emotions. I strongly recommend group therapy to my clients: Group provides a safe place in which to discuss those problems with which we grapple alone. Sometimes friendships established in group blossom into long-term relationships.

And those friendships can be healing. Two clients of mine, for instance, hard-boiled two dozen eggs and drew on them the faces or names of persons with whom they were angry, went to a Seattle park one evening, and threw the eggs at rocks as they yelled out their angers.

But I'm not sure I'd suggest others do the same: My clients were unlucky. An enterprising police officer happened along, caught them in the act, and arrested them for disturbing the peace! To be sure, anger released in violence is counter-productive, and violent anger provides neither "release" nor peace to the avenger. Unless a person confronts and works through the original *causes* of anger, the violence will only become repetitive.

Fred, for example, can't maintain a stable relationship. Though he wants marriage and children, each union inevitably dissolves when he becomes violent. His sorrow each time is sincere; yet his resolve never to repeat his violence inevitably breaks down in time. As a child, Fred suffered years of abuse from his parents. He has, of course, never confronted them, never attempted to discover the reasons, never tried to resolve his own anger. He is perpetually condemned, therefore, to act out that anger over and over.

Yet, anger does have its place. The emotion of anger, for instance, can make us physically stronger should we face physical attack. Because the manager who normally opened the store was out of town, one client of mine found herself walking down the street at 5:30 a.m. to unlock the store in which she worked as a clerk.

A man started walking beside her.

"Holdup," he said softly.

She thought he'd said, "How are you?" and replied, "Fine. How are you?"

"Holdup," he repeated, and stuck something that felt like a gun in her side. "Give me your purse."

But she couldn't, because the store keys were inside. Nobody else was in sight. So, with a loud scream, she hit him hard over the head with her loaded purse. He was so astonished he took off like a frightened rabbit.

My timid client was so amazed at her own outburst of anger that she almost fainted. But she did not. The woman rallied, ran to the store, opened it, and locked herself inside before collapsing in fear.

Anger enables us to protect loved ones, to demand rights as persons, to promote justice for those who are exploited. Thus, anger generates energy within, which serves to mobilize us for attack: Muscles tighten, our pulse speeds up, our blood pressure rises.

When those physiological reactions are ignored, and ignored repeatedly, serious health problems can result: headaches, irritability, insomnia, depression, a general weariness, arthritis. Anger, then, is legitimately used only when it leads to some kind of healthy, honest result.

The very religious, in particular, may have real difficulty expressing anger. Such persons may have long heard anger called a sin, but without a distinction having been made between the feelings of anger and the violent expressionsof anger. As my examples illustrate, repressing, stuffing, or ignoring anger also results in harmful effects.

When Jesus entered the Temple and found the House of God had been violated by buying and selling – the exchange of money – He got angry. His physiological impulses kicked in, and Jesus drove the buyers and sellers away.

If we learned to behave in an upfront manner, and if we could pass on that technique to our children, then repressed anger might no longer create adult children who long to be held, lonesome elderly adults who are unable to fall back on resources within because there are none, talented individuals who are crippled in the use of their gifts, depressed men and women who are overcome with inexplicable sadness, addicts who have no idea how they got that way.

Occasionally, when people ask me what I do, I tell them, "I teach people how to get angry." That's as good a description of therapy as any one short sentence can offer.

"Be angry," St. Paul wrote, "but do not sin" (Eph. 4:26).

SUMMARY

God created us. Then, God looked upon us – the resultant handiwork – and declared us good. A big part of the human package
that makes us who we are, our emotions are likewise good things.
But we often need to learn how to handle our emotions. Among
the most powerful of the emotions is anger. It's one of the most
difficult, too – both to handle, and to control.

Highlights

- Uncontrolled anger is dangerous, but not even God begrudges
  us the gift of properly channeled, responsibly expressed anger.
- Sometimes, unresolved anger is turned inward. When that happens, we harm *ourselves* – not the people toward whom we feel
  the anger.
- Coming to terms with anger often requires that we accept our
  feelings, including feelings of anger, and name the roots or
  causes of our anger.

Discussion

1. What are some ways that people inappropriately express anger?
2. How does unresolved anger hurt us?
3. Name some "safe" ways to express anger? Why are they safe?
   Why are they useful?
4. What is the significance of a support network in handling
   anger? List three people you consider to be a part of your
   support network. How might one of these persons help you
   now?

SIX

Say Goodbye to
Self-Destructive Behavior

Nancy lived for some years with a husband whose physical brutality put her in the hospital a number of times. Eventually she worked up the courage to divorce Jed. Several years later, though, he was stranded without a place to live – unless he paid for it – for a couple of months before he embarked on a long trip.

Now, Nancy's ex was by no means destitute. In fact, he had thousands of dollars, and Nancy knew that. Nevertheless, when the man asked Nancy if he could stay in her apartment she said, "Of course. Yes. Certainly."

Naturally, he brought along his possessions and clothes. He couldn't live without his personal property, could he? And so his things, too, were stuffed into Nancy's one-bedroom apartment. Nancy had not expected his *furniture*. But she was eager to *accommodate* him. She imparted to me that she realized her ex ought to store his furniture and at least take responsibility for storage costs. But she found herself unable to tell him that. He, meanwhile, was sleeping in her living room.

This man was extremely abusive to Nancy emotionally. Indeed, before he moved out he stole her jewelry and other small objects of value.

Though Nancy knew these items were in his suitcases the day before he left, she could not bring herself to take them out in his absence. Some were very valuable: one necklace, a gift, was valued at $3,000.

My clients often exhibit self-defeating behaviors. Overwhelming fear of failure, for instance, may stall success before it begins; genuine success may be stymied by a false sense of "I'm faking it"; inferiority fears may block one's ability to pull off a top-level performance; fear of rejection may restrain persons from utilizing initiative; fear and feelings of self-unworthiness may transfer into self-defeating behaviors that may ensure a client gets no promotions. And then there are the personal inhibiting behaviors: shyness, procrastination, anxiety, depression, fatigue, addictions, social withdrawal. The list goes on and on.

It's important to point out, however, that persons bogged down with these kinds of problems can help themselves by figuring out where the self-defeating behaviors started, how they are perpetuated, which behaviors are specific to themselves, and how they can be replaced.

In fact, Nancy herself could hardly believe her own behavior. So we delved into her childhood. It turned out that Nancy had been abused by two young uncles for several years. Her mother stood up for her own brothers, however, and refused to hear of any bad behavior on their part. Thus, Nancy had no recourse but to submit to their cruelty. Fighting them only invited more aggression. And so she learned in childhood – when repeated behaviors imprint themselves on the brain – to let men do whatever they want.

Now, this submissive acceptance of pain and maltreatment had enabled Nancy to cope as a child. But as an adult, the same behavior was seriously self-defeating. Why, I asked, had she not reported Jed's action to the police? Why had she not extracted the stolen goods from his suitcases and stood them outside her apartment door? Why had she not changed her locks so Jed couldn't gain entrance?

Nancy could only respond that she feared he would beat her. Or he might kill her, as he had threatened in the past. I pointed out that she could have reported him to the police and gotten a restraining order; or she could have left the apartment and stayed with friends for a few days since Jed would soon be leaving town. Ruefully she agreed. But Nancy's childhood experiences were clearly engraved in her mind, and she'd reacted with the same submissive behavior she'd practiced as an abused child.

In general, self-defeating behaviors are learned in childhood. As noted, at that time they enable the individual to cope with difficult situations. But later they are mindlessly repeated by the child-adult in new encounters, and it is here that they often prove inappropriate, even damaging.

Nancy, of course, had not come to see me because of the above problems. The symptoms from which she sought relief were depression: weeping for hours at a time; and eating – Nancy was piling on pounds.

As a child Nancy had experienced food as one of her few pleasures, and had often spent hours weeping. Now, in a time of emotional turmoil, she fell back on the old coping mechanisms. Early childhood experiences had been so devastating she had learned never to trust. Yet, even as she sat before me, Nancy was transferring that learning onto the entire adult world. That she could trust a therapist long enough to ask for help represented a major step forward.

Many people fall back on old patterns of self-destructive behavior at critical times in life. (And these individuals do so regardless of how bright and self-sufficient they are.) But the one certain result of self-defeating behavior is that it delivers the exact result the individual tries to avoid.

Nancy, for example, wanted to better herself. And she had even started college. Then, however, she dropped out.

"My mother said I would never succeed at anything," she wept.

It took some time, but in the end Nancy *did* return to school; and she did graduate. But first she had to figure out why – and how – she was unconsciously tripping herself up with previously learned behavior patterns.

Clients frequently ask, "Why do I act this way? Why don't things turn out right? What's wrong with me?" But when therapists try, slowly and gently, to help them change the self-defeating behavior, we professionals are likely to meet resistance. Clients have acted out of a faulty belief system most of their lives; change is scary and threatening. My first objective, therefore, is to help clients understand why they choose behaviors that can't possibly bring success and happiness.

Jenny, another of my clients, entered therapy because she had completed studies for her Ph.D., had compiled the requisite research data – but could *not* write her dissertation. She had struggled with her inability to put the material together for six years, had obtained as many delays as the University would allow, and now had only six months left to complete her paper. *And she could not do it.*

She couldn't write the dissertation because she had a small child at home. Could she afford child-care? Yes, easily. But she *enjoyed* spending time with her child. Eventually, though, Jenny did agree to put her child in day-care provided by the University for three hours daily until she finished her dissertation.

But at the next session, Jenny explained that she couldn't write at home because she kept thinking of all the odds and ends of jobs that needed to be done around the house, and she couldn't devote her attention to the dissertation when that happened.

What kind of jobs? Well, you know, taking out the garbage, straightening up the attic, painting the washroom, baking cookies and pies. Finally, Jenny agreed to set aside two hours a day during which she would do nothing more than sit before her computer and write her dissertation.

At the next session, however, no writing had been done. She still could think of nothing except various household chores.

Could Jenny write at the school? Well, yes, but it would have to be arranged.

Yet at the next session, Jenny was still in the process of *arranging* for the use of a computer for a few hours daily at her university.

Throughout therapy, we looked at the underlying reasons for the continued failure to write the dissertation. As we delved into her childhood, it surfaced that as a child Jenny had suffered from chronic nosebleeds. In school and elsewhere, her nose might start bleeding at any time, and this embarrassed Jenny.

At home, clothing and bedsheets might get blood on them – which annoyed her mother very much. Only after she passed through fifth grade did Jenny's parents bring her to a physician who successfully treated the problem. Did the other kids at school make fun of her? Well, yes. Why didn't her parents bring her to a doctor earlier? They had expected she would grow out of it.

Did her parents blame her for the nosebleeds, accuse her of doing something to set them off? Oh, yes. With some frequency. Her mother was angry and scolded her, but it happened again and again nevertheless.

Jenny's significant developmental years were scarred with helplessness, pain, humiliation, and failure. Neither of her parents had attended college, nor had her siblings. Now that a Ph.D. was within her grasp, she couldn't allow herself such marked success. All through life she had struggled to win the approval of her parents – and never got it. If she won a doctorate, thereby achieving success, she would abandon all hope of acceptance by her family. Why continue a quest to a bad end?

The lifelong fear of losing her parents' approval – approval Jenny had never actually experienced – crippled the young woman. Unconsciously Jenny said to herself, "If I get a Ph.D. and thus behave so differently from my family, they will cut me off." The failure to complete her dissertation, however, would produce the very result she tried to avoid: Instead, the family could say, "See, Jenny, we said you'd end up a failure." (In time, Jenny *did* earn her Ph.D.)

To change her negative self-defeating behaviors, though, Jenny first had to understand and recognize her underlying fears. Generally speaking, people who come to me for help don't want to do this because they will face within themselves sub-personalities that they don't like: an inadequate person, a passive-aggressive person, a conformist, a weak and vulnerable person, a rebel, a joker, an addict, an agitator. Of all my clients who exhibit self-defeating behaviors, I must say the majority are afraid of one thing and one thing only: success.

Most persons who come to me for therapy have already begun to accept some responsibility for their self-defeating behaviors, but that doesn't mean they want to abandon them. They will bring the dysfunctional behavior to the therapy session, agree with insights suggested, resolve to avoid this particular trap – and then go out and repeat the behavior all over again.

Here's an example: Leona is an engineer, and an extremely capable one. She is the kind of engineer who runs boilers, takes valves apart, repairs refrigeration, and so on. Usually she is the only woman engaged in her workplace, and knows that she may be the victim of gender discrimination. After she started the job in her present workplace – a big and well-known hospital – she felt keenly that co-workers did not acknowledge her presence, that her good performance got no recognition, and that she was unfairly dismissed rather than complimented and affirmed for her professional competence.

Gradually and slowly, in therapy, Leona achieved insight. She had grown up in a dysfunctional home in which she wasn't touched, certainly never hugged or noticed. Her parents were not mean, just so consumed by their own severe personal problems that they lacked the ability to care for their children apart from feeding and clothing them. So Leona grew up invisible and angry. Now, unconsciously, she was repeating the invisible behavior.

As an engineer she carefully slipped around, in and out, did her work, but struggled to avoid attention. Nobody complimented her at work because she took care that nobody saw her. And, as in childhood, she was furious. But she did come to realize that she schemed to keep herself invisible in the workplace. So Leona changed her behavior. Day by day she worked at joking with co-workers, asking for assistance when necessary, becoming a member of the group.

The first step toward triumphing over self-defeating behavior is to take notice of it. Nobody can change behavior until he or she at least knows about it.

Julie, for instance, kept everything under control. Her childhood home and family was characterized by so much chaos that Julie had learned early on to maintain control in her own sphere. As she matured, of course, the sphere got bigger and bigger. Gradually she controlled her own family, her marriage, her children, her work. In keeping with the need to control she became a management consultant, and an excellent one. Control and order are the fields Julie knew best, but her personal relationships were suffering. By the time Julie came to see me, she actually had identified her problem behavior.

Most clients are not this advanced. Some ask how to figure out their own self-defeating behavior. My suggestion, if you want to do what Julie did, is this: Ask others for feedback. A note of caution here, though. If you're asking somebody in your family of origin for feedback, do so with care. Because dysfunctional behaviors often are learned early on in the family, family members may evidence the same kind of self-defeating behavior that you do. When that's the case, they may not be able to recognize troublesome habits any more than you can. And the same might be true with friends if you find yourself in the company of people with life patterns similar to yours. So, in all cases, make this step carefully if at all.

As you invite feedback from others, ask yourself: Are these individuals leading healthy, happy lives – free from destructive behavior patterns? Even so, if what you hear from friends and others who know you well does not agree with your own sense of self, get a second opinion. And remember: Sometimes we do have to face unpleasant facts.

Finally, examine those times in your life when you felt the most down, depressed, blue. Try to recall what kind of behavior was exhibited during these low times. Compulsive overeating? Heavy drinking? Shy and unassuming behavior? Fighting and quarrelling? Manipulating those around you? Withdrawing from social engagements?

Then, examine those periods during which you felt most happy and fulfilled, and consider how you behaved during those periods.

If you still don't have a clear sense of how you might practice self-destructive behavior, it may be wise to find a mental health counselor and sign up for a few sessions.

To truly improve your life, you will need to change the self-defeating behavior. And this will not be easy. I can reassure you, though, that many people have taken on such challenges and – to their delight – succeeded.

My client, Alice, was one of them. Alice was engaged in employment far below her ability and level of professional training. This came to light when Alice talked about how difficult it was to get by on her meager salary.

"You're capable of much more," I pointed out. Alice had a master's degree, after all, and had been engaged as a psychiatric nurse. Worn out by that position, she had resigned and was now working as a typist.

"Have you ever gotten a promotion in your present employment?" I asked.

"I couldn't," she said. "My supervisor needs me."

"Why?"

"Well, I train in each new person who comes, and I make sure everybody's work for that day is completed."

"Have any of the persons you've trained been promoted?"

"Oh, yes."

"Why are you doing a supervisor's job without a supervisor's pay?"

As Alice thought it over, she realized, slowly, that her supervisor was taking advantage of her. Alice was, in effect, in the taking-care-of-everybody-except-myself mode. It took time, but Alice eventually requested a promotion. Of course she got it – along with a raise.

With more therapy and more encouragement, Alice was able to search for a different job. (She also had feared that she might be unable to locate work other than the lowly position she had fallen into.) But she did find better work, work as a medical secretary with a much higher rate of compensation. She had made the transition.

Additional suggestions for overcoming self-defeating behavior: People need to be willing to risk failure. Change is always scary. Perhaps failures will occur. But failure need not be the end; it might be the beginning. Everybody can learn from mistakes. Persons ought to investigate the root of their failure, hunt for alternative solutions, and take corrective action.

Then, too, the possibility of rejection always looms large when persons institute changes. But rejection might be the necessary prerequisite to success: It may teach us what we are called to change. People can overcome the fear of failure attached to life's challenges by understanding that everybody fails sometime. Further, we can learn to use adversity as a motivational tool, learn to confront challenges with wisdom and persistence.

Talent alone does not guarantee success. Success requires determination, dedication, courage in the face of failure, and a willingness to explore other possibilities.

Attitudes that prevent people from realizing their potential may result from blaming previous negative experiences for present difficulties while refusing to deal with old problems. Success is an act of measuring the process of attaining one's goals, rather than a tangible thing to be achieved or an identification that must be made. To this end, an optimistic attitude is helpful.

Focusing on one's strengths is more important than dwelling on one's weaknesses. We might keep in mind, too, that in the long run average people often do better in life than people with higher intelligence because ordinary people can be more disciplined and patient in achieving their goals, and thus may become more successful than fast-trackers.

When all is said and done, the trait most important to success is perseverance. People determined to succeed do not give up easily. They turn rejection, adversity, and misfortune into opportunities. Generally speaking, everyone who hangs in there long enough wins.

SUMMARY

Self-defeating behaviors are actions and/or behaviors we practice over and over that keep us from those people, places, and things we really want in life. In overcoming these behaviors, we need to figure out where they started, why they are perpetuated, and how we might replace them with more productive habits.

Highlights

- Self-defeating behaviors take root during childhood. They are learned.

- In times of crisis, we are particularly vulnerable to falling back on negative behavior patterns, further complicating the challenges at hand.

- Changing behaviors requires us to first understand and recognize our underlying fears and other triggers of these negative behaviors.

- Feedback from trusted, emotionally healthy others can help us better evaluate ourselves, our relationships, and our behaviors.

Discussion

1. What are some ways we might notice or become more aware of our self-defeating behaviors?

2. What self-defeating behaviors, or repeated negative actions, have we experienced in ourselves – or in our families? (Behavior of parents/other relatives, particularly brothers and sisters?)

3. How might we set about changing our own behavior? Might a therapist or family counselor help us help ourselves change self-defeating behaviors?

4. Why is a willingness to risk failure crucial for changing self-defeating behaviors?

SEVEN

Sweet Forgiveness

Forgiveness is not a willed act. We cannot command forgiveness, neither from ourselves nor from others. Indeed, coercion by others to forgive is unchristian and can be seriously harmful to the individual ordered to produce forgiveness.

The first step we need to take toward forgiveness, then, is to accept ourselves as we are – and that's much more difficult than it sounds. After that, we can work on accepting others as they are. Bill Wilson, one founder of Alcoholics Anonymous, wrote, "Our very first problem is to accept our present circumstances as they are, ourselves as we are, and the people about us as they are. This is to adopt a realistic humility without which no genuine advance can even begin." Humility is not easily achieved.

Most important, though, is this little-understood fact: Forgiveness is not for the benefit of that person who inflicted the injury. The persons who hurt us are responsible for the quality of their own personal lives and for taking the necessary steps toward their own personal healing. Forgiveness must benefit the person who forgives. That's why my clients struggle so fiercely to forgive, why they weep for forgiveness. If only they could forgive, they reason, it would be all over, and they could get on with their lives and put the past behind them. Painful as it is, this yearning for forgiveness is a prerequisite. Always, we long to forgive before we achieve forgiveness.

I have worked with clients in Canada, Australia, and New Zealand, as well as in the United States, who struggle with forgiveness. And in that time, I have learned that forgiveness of those injuries inflicted by persons with whom we are intimate and whom we count among our nearest and dearest – injuries that shatter a person's idea of morality and attack one's most fundamental belief system – is very difficult.

When men and women come to me with the inevitable problems and questions about forgiveness as they struggle through therapy, I tell them to *forget* forgiveness. Leave it alone. Trust God, and leave forgiveness alone.

Scripture deals with forgiveness in a variety of ways. For example, when the Pharisees wanted to "catch" Jesus, they waited until he came into their little town. Then they dragged before him a woman who had been caught in adultery. "Shall we stone her according to the Law?" they asked. Now, should Jesus say no, they had a pious Jew who advocated breaking Mosaic Law. Should Jesus say yes, they had somebody who was not living the mercy he preached.

But Jesus was ready for them: "Let the man among you who has no sin," Christ admonished, "throw the first stone." Then he bent and wrote on the ground with his finger. One by one the men dropped their stones and slipped silently away.

Next, Jesus asks the woman if anyone has condemned her. Of course, nobody has; they've all gone. He doesn't condemn her either, but sends her off in peace with the gentle admonition, "And sin no more."

Has he asked her to forgive the would-be murderers panting for her blood? To forgive them for dragging her before him? No.

And what about the thief dying with Jesus on the cross? If forgiveness is so all-important, why doesn't Jesus ask whether he has forgiven his executioners and those who have hurt him throughout life? Here again, not a word about forgiveness. Jesus simply promises the man that "this day" he will enter Paradise. So not even Jesus considered forgiveness to be a condition of salvation. Rather, it is necessary *for Jesus to forgive us.*

From a psychotherapeutic perspective, forgiveness means *not forgetting.* Said psychiatrist Thomas Szasz, "The stupid neither forgive nor forget; the naive forgive and forget; the wise forgive, but they do not forget."

"To forgive and forget," observed the German philosopher Schopenhauer, "means to throw away dearly bought experience."

"Forgetting can be dangerous," adds Lewis Smedes, professor of theology and ethics at Fuller Theological Seminary in Pasadena, Ca. "To forget is to repress and deny what happened. To forget opens the self up to getting walloped again."

Too often those persons who seek my professional help have struggled fiercely to forgive, stuffed the pain, forced themselves to forget, tormented themselves into a dangerous repression of memories. Consequently, those repressed memories lie buried in the unconscious, slowly building a power as big as an atom bomb – and just as damaging to the human psyche. In other words, repressed memories can be fearfully destructive. With sorrow I watch clients who've forced themselves to forget. What they don't know is that the unconscious *never* forgets.

Too often we do not like ourselves as we are, nor others as they are. Nevertheless, we should not resign ourselves to intolerable circumstances. Before we forgive the "unforgivable," we are called to look at ourselves and our situations and say, honestly, "Yes. This is the way it truly is. I've done bad things, others have done bad things to me, and I've ended up a mess – but I don't have to stay this way."

We don't have to like what we see, but if we want to heal, we must at least see it. The endeavor to be truly honest is the requisite first step of the long, long journey to forgiveness.

Frequently those who have been hurt and abused, especially if this happens in childhood, adopt self-destructive behavior patterns or wreak destruction on others. Acceptance does not mean approval. It doesn't mean throw in the towel and quit, either. It doesn't mean adjust to the intolerable.

Acceptance means, first of all, accepting ourselves. We may moan and weep at the pain others have inflicted . . . and simultaneously inflict even worse pain on ourselves. Too many of us hate ourselves, and hug that hate close to our hearts. We don't believe we hate ourselves, but we can't make the journey to forgiveness without facing the facts. Maybe I'm too short or too tall, too fat or too lean, too dark or too blond. Maybe I'm not talented or smart enough.

Only after we accept ourselves as we are – sins and all – can we begin the journey toward loving ourselves. After we have learned to love our imperfect selves, after we have become able to give compassion to ourselves, we can love and offer compassion to others.

When Jesus was asked to name the two greatest commandments he replied, love God above all things and love your neighbor as yourself.

Within that response lies buried a pearl many of us never discover: God *expects* us to love ourselves. And, sadly, most of us don't. For almost 30 years I was principal of schools to which juvenile courts sent teenagers adjudicated delinquent. Over and over I saw those frightened angry teens abuse themselves. After all, drug and alcohol abuse are, deep-down, ways of hurting ourselves. Unless our parents have unselfishly loved us and modeled that love for us, it's extremely difficult to love ourselves. But we need to learn how.

And to help us along this hard and painful path, we need to learn something else: how to pray. The first words of the Divine Office, sung several times a day by members of religious Orders, are, *"Oh, God, come to my assistance . . . Oh, Lord, hasten to help me."* We too can breathe those few short words many times a day. Prayer heals brokenness . . . and the seriously injured are shattered indeed.

Unfortunately, adults abused as children tend to replicate the abusive experience throughout their lives.

Take Dee, for example. Dee was a brilliant young woman in her 30s who came to me because she attended community college, desired enough education to obtain a good job, but was convinced she could not learn. She was also a recovering alcoholic. Her father had, when she was a teenager, brought her outdoors on Saturdays to work with him, but brought no food. Around 2 p.m., he'd send her to buy a case of beer, and he'd offer cans to her. When Dee came to see me, she was already in recovery.

For an entire year, though, our weekly sessions followed the same routine and went no further: Dee met me, burst into tears, recounted a class incident in which she could not answer a question directed to her; always, she knew the answer but was too frightened to give it. Other times, she'd failed to ask for clarification because she'd been so scared that she'd lost her voice.

On the first day of each quarter, in fact, Dee had remained in bed all day, crying, because she was too scared to face new classmates and new professors. Then, she wept also over her grades – usually all As – because she was convinced that she was stupid. The professors, Dee believed, had pitied and passed her. Dee's most copious tears of all, however, occurred the day the college gave her a scholarship. She needed it because she was working her way through, but certain that she did not deserve it, Dee looked on the scholarship as confirmation of her assumption that the professors pitied her.

As we discussed Dee's childhood, a story of bitter pain emerged. Her father, a police officer and later an assistant district attorney, had held nightly sessions with her over school work. He would question, question, and question Dee until she made the inevitable mistake. Then the punishment would begin: She might be ordered to kneel in a corner for an hour without leaning on any support; if she slumped, she would be ordered to begin the hour again. She might be beaten. She might be ordered to eat old cereal with dead ants in it. These sessions continued night after night, year after year.

Gradually, through counseling, Dee came to realize that she *could* learn. With some recognition of her abilities came a fierce anger at her parents and siblings. The more clearly she perceived the lies with which she had been raised, the more furious she became. But as a Catholic raised in a "good Catholic home," she felt she ought to forgive – and she could not.

Dee's father had divorced her mother, remarried, and moved out of the area. And still Dee hated him; she hated them all.

It took three years of therapy for Dee to accept her brilliance, to experience the thrill of learning, the joy of acquiring insights. When finally she accepted *herself*, when she admitted that the professors did not pity her, when she qualified for her degree in social work, when she learned to be compassionate to herself, Dee discovered, gently, how to forgive.

For her graduation she invited her family. Dee knows who she is now, and she forgives gracefully, amazed at herself and how far she has come.

And then there is Sherry's story. Sherry drove a long distance to Columbus, Ohio, where I was scheduled to give a workshop in order to meet me. She knew, Sherry told me, that she could never forgive her mother. What her mother had said and done to her as a child, Sherry explained, was beyond human ability to forgive.

Sherry's stepfather had sexually abused both seven-year old Sherry and her twin sister. When they told their mother, she asked, "How could you *let* him do that to you?" Then, for punishment, she sent them to bed without dinner. She never discussed the subject again.

As she sat in my office, Sherry embarked on a long and winding road to recovery from inner pain and shame. Progress was slow: seven years, much longer than usual, in my professional experience.

All the while, though, Sherry, like so many others, worried about forgiveness. Finally, I asked her to *forget* forgiveness and concentrate on the journey. As the months dragged slowly by, Sherry often wept with pain, and questioned me repeatedly as to whether she could ever recover. Many more months elapsed, all of them months of pain. Sherry relocated and entered therapy with another counselor; and still, even as the rest of her shattered life healed and mended, Sherry wondered if she could ever achieve total healing, achieve forgiveness.

Then one day Sherry phoned long-distance. And even across those many miles, I could hear the incredulity in her voice. "You know what?" she was saying. "I've forgiven her! I don't know when it happened, or how. I'm just not angry anymore." No person was more surprised than Sherry.

Finally, she could visit her mother. The two had the first real talk of their lives.

I was not totally surprised. I have observed this scenario unfold again and again. A person who is serious about his or her healing will, when healed, automatically forgive. During the course of therapy Sherry had screamed out her anger, confronted it, faced her demons. As she explored buried pains, Sherry was caught up in emotional turmoil, confusion, guilt. But as she gradually surrendered her denial system, discussed her repressions, these lost their awesome power over her.

Underneath the torrents of our anger and fury lie tremendous strengths that cannot be loosed until the conflicting emotions have been worked through and resolved. Once the self-blaming, self-downgrading had ceased, Sherry was able to accept and love herself as she is. Then, she was able to begin genuinely loving others. When finally she achieved peace and tranquility enough to forgive herself for her own self-destructiveness, self-blaming, and impossible self-demands for perfection, then Sherry could forgive others, love them, and open lines for communication.

Perhaps with Dee's story, and with Sherry's, we can better understand that forgiveness is not an event.We can't simply make up our minds to forgive, do so, and have it all be over. Forgiveness is a process, and a long one.

An old spiritual tale illustrates the nature of forgiveness well: A disciple asked a certain Rabbi how one should pray for forgiveness and was told to observe the behavior of a certain innkeeper before Yom Kippur. According to this parable, told by E. Kurtz and K. Ketcham in *The Spirituality of Imperfection*, the disciple took a room at the inn but saw nothing unusual about the innkeeper. On the night before Yom Kippur, however, the disciple saw the man open two big ledgers. From one, the innkeeper read aloud all the sins he had committed during the past year. From the other, he read all the bad things that had happened. Then he began to pray.

"Dear God," the innkeeper said, "it is true I have sinned against You. But You have done many distressful things to me too.

"We are now beginning a new year. Let us wipe the slate clean. I will forgive You, and You forgive me."

Forgiveness is a many-splendored, but crooked and curved stairway to the vision of God.

SUMMARY

We are not obligated to forgive those who have hurt us. Indeed, forgiveness – in itself – cannot put the past behind us. What is more, coercing somebody to forgive those who have hurt him or her can be quite harmful to the injured individual if that person is not psychologically ready to forgive.

Highlights

- The first step on the road to forgiveness is acceptance – acceptance of ourselves as we are, and of others as they are.
- Forgiveness is not for the benefit of the person who inflicted injury. Forgiveness, properly practiced, is for the benefit of the injured.
- Not even Jesus compels us to forgive always as a condition of salvation.
- Above all, forgiveness doesn't just happen. Forgiveness is a process, and it can be a long one.

Discussion

1. Forgiveness means *not* forgetting. Why can forgetting be dangerous?
2. What role does acceptance – of ourselves, of our situation, and of others – play in forgiveness?
3. How can loving ourselves protect us from those who might hurt us? How does the process of learning to love ourselves relate to the forgiveness process?

EIGHT

Eating Your Problems Away?

"I can't stop eating," seriously overweight clients often tell me. "I know I'm putting on too much weight, but I can't quit." Or they'll say: "I've got high blood pressure and my doctor told me to lose weight. But I can't." Still others report, "I've gone on lots of diets, but I gain it all back again."

Clients who must lose weight because of health problems frequently pay good money – lots of it – on diets and weight loss programs and still they're grossly overweight. One young woman, at least 100 pounds too heavy, told me she had already spent enough on diets to have traveled three times around Europe on the money.

I meet clients ashamed to take a walk because they're self-conscious about their weight. Clients wearing clothes too tight because they've spent so much on weight loss they can't afford new attire. Clients who enjoy swimming but won't because they dread appearing in public in a swimsuit.

I've had clients tell me they can't take a taste of ice cream; one taste, and they pick up a huge spoon and sit there until they have finished the entire gallon. Some get up during the night to eat. A few clients can't shop in ordinary grocery stores because they're too large to maneuver the aisles. Still others can't get jobs because nobody will hire grossly overweight persons. And I've got clients who don't get physicals because they know physicians will shake their heads in dismay about the overweight.

Most of us know that diets don't work. Ninety-five percent of those who go on diets regain the weight and usually more. Nevertheless, the diet industry advertises very aggressively because there's money in diets: about $35 billion a year. And so desperate people continue to reach out for every new diet, every new diet book, even though the last ten diets have failed.

Jeanette is a client who experienced all these problems, and overcame them. From her story several principles of reasonable weight control can be developed.

Initially, Jeanette sought therapy for severe childhood abuse: sexual, emotional, and physical. Her life had, until the past few years, been a nightmare.

"I don't even know why I ate seven candy bars," she told me one day, describing her latest binge. "I don't even like that kind of candy, and I wasn't hungry. But I couldn't stop."

Jeanette had been thin most of her life. She had, in fact, modeled successfully for several years. To maintain the body shape requisite for models, she had fasted on liquids for weeks at a time or taken extremely heavy doses of laxatives. She remembered that as a child she occasionally ate paste in school to the horror of teachers and students, or nibbled on hay along the roadside. She wasn't hungry then, either. She simply needed to eat.

After Jeanette had put on more than 100 pounds while in therapy, I asked her to see a physician to rule out the dangers of high blood pressure and diabetes. Since everything Jeanette does, she does perfectly, she saw not one but two physicians. Each gave the same prescription: "Forget about fat. Continue in therapy. When your personal problems are resolved, the weight will drop off." Both Jeanette and I were relieved; we already knew her compulsive eating resulted from a seriously dysfunctional childhood. Now we had a green light to focus on therapy alone to heal her.

Persons who eat in the hopeless attempt to fill a bottomless hole inside can expect to fail on commercial diets. Why? Because they hear the same commands they heard as a child: "Don't eat this. Don't eat that. And don't mess up again. Don't. Don't. Don't."

Eventually the adult-child rebels as the growing-child could not: He or she breaks the diet. He or she binges. Or purges. Yet, all the while, the empty hole inside keeps gnawing through the resolve – and then the shamed individual speeds off into another eating spree which packs all the pounds back on again, and more. Perhaps the adults who once scolded the child are no longer around, so the child now takes over for them: "You're hopeless," the adult-child screams at him- or herself. "You've screwed up again. Can't you ever learn!" More depressed than before, he or she now eats even more to blot out the pain.

That's what Jeanette did, over and over again.

And that's certainly what Mary, who quit alcohol and then turned to food, did. "I eat a gallon of ice cream at a time," she told me ruefully.

So I explained that where she had once deadened her pain with alcohol, she now deadened it with food. (For most grossly overweight persons, food is as much of an addiction as alcohol and drugs.)

For her part, Jeanette gradually learned in therapy that the adults she once trembled before no longer rule her life. She learned how to change their voices instead of turning them into her own. She realized her mother would like her no better now if she were thin – simply because the woman had liked her daughter no more when she was a model.

She could, Jeanette finally realized, emerge from the hopelessness and despair she had experienced in her growing-up family, even though that called for a long therapeutic walk through a shaded valley. Because now Jeanette had the support of a therapist. Now she was also in group therapy and had the support of the group. Now Jeanette could glimpse hope.

For all of us, compulsive thinking about food can keep our minds off present concerns and past problems. While we argue with ourselves about what we are or are not going to eat, we forget the harsh words a boss might have uttered or a friend might have spilled in exasperation. We stop thinking about financial problems. We can't obsess over past years, endlessly questioning how we might have made them more productive, how we could have won a more satisfying love from our parents in childhood. Food compulsions do have their rewards; that's why we cling to them. But their long-term effects are deadly.

We'd do far better facing the pain and dealing constructively with it. Americans experience a variety of problems at work: overbearing supervisors, bosses who use office time to do off-the-job work, co-workers who dump their problems on us, a demanding, ever-changing workplace with computer updates occurring constantly. And on and on.

As a therapist I help clients recognize the real pain, the pain they don't want to see, don't want to deal with. And then, we search out ways of coping.

The first thing we need to recognize is that pain is a part of life. We might love the work we do, but at times its demands are overpowering. We love our children, but occasionally long for a few days to ourselves. Merely pushing such pain and stress out of consciousness, though, is dangerous. These things need to be faced. When we obsess about food, diets, what to eat and what not, we may manage to avoid facing our reality for a little while. The obsessive focus on food, however, brings its own pain: the binge eating, perhaps purging, the expense, the self-blaming, the added weight.

And not all problems can be resolved. If, for instance, care of the environment is a primary concern – and it's obviously not given top priority on a global basis – then I need to discover how to enjoy happiness regardless. *My grief will not make the environment better.* I make the world a better place by achieving happiness for myself. I make the globe more gentle by developing a gentle lifestyle for myself.

After clients have explored the causes of their pain, the pain they ate to avoid, and searched out healthy coping styles, then we hunt out paths to happiness.

Candy, for instance, loved to give workshops but found little opportunity in her own city. So she hooked up with an agency – an effort that requires work – and now she currently flies throughout the U.S. presenting workshops. Candy totally enjoys herself, and is losing weight effortlessly.

Judy quit a good job because it required full-time work on weekends, and quickly found another with free weekends. She lost almost a hundred pounds.

Violet lost a job she loved. In her grief she picked up writing. Now she has sold several books and lost the weight that plagued her throughout life.

These are only a few of my clients. All learned, eventually, that happiness is a gift of God, but we do have to stretch ourselves to achieve it. If food and eating are our primary sources of happiness, we are seriously deprived. We can help ourselves, perhaps, by asking ourselves some questions:

- What would I really like to do?
- What would make me happy?
- What do I enjoy?
- What can I do about it?

When Jeanette asked herself those questions, she acknowledged that her supervisor at work was irrational and unbearable. Then, she discussed the situation with the local head of her company. He stated that Jeanette's work was excellent, and the company did not want to lose her. Consequently, her job and her supervisor were changed.

But complaining was a big step for Jeanette. She feared she might lose her position, or that everybody in the office would be angry. Instead, Jeanette no longer eats seven candy bars at work with no comprehension of why she swallows them when she isn't hungry and doesn't enjoy the taste. The compulsion is gone.

Jeanette recognized her fears and faced them. Only then was she able to conquer them. For a long time, her husband had wanted to move into a more picturesque location of town. Money was no problem. But Jeanette thought she needed the security of the same old place, felt afraid to move, to go into new surroundings. Once she discussed the problems, they lost much of their terror. Now Jeanette loves her new home. It's one more step on her path to a happy life.

Jeanette quit weighing herself, too. When she moved, she left the scales behind. The morning weigh-in was a daily ordeal that she dreaded but felt compelled to do. Today, a few pounds on or off are no longer a big deal. Jeanette now is weighed only when she sees her doctor – and she's losing.

Jeanette accepted as well that she could no longer relate to her family or origin. Conversations, phone calls, letters – all brought back the childhood pain and terror, and all drove her to eat in a futile effort to kill the memories. So she simply terminated relationships with her family. (Several clients have recognized this kind of necessity. Sometimes healing comes later, sometimes never. But there are times when we have to admit what we can't handle, and move on.)

Instead of looking to family, Jeanette turned to God, finding peace and consolation in frequent prayer. Problems no longer loom big and forbidding; now, God is in her life. "I pray several times daily," Jeanette says.

Finally, Jeanette works constructively in therapy. She's unflinchingly honest, searching for the roots of her problems. I would guess that, for seriously overweight clients, therapy is more productive than diets, and the results are more likely to be lasting.

Therapists can't do the work, though. We can only point out the road to wholeness and happiness.

As Jeanette slowly loses weight, she's neither dieting nor making any attempt to do so. One day in the not-too-distant future, she will regain her figure and look as lovely on the outside as she is within.

SUMMARY

Persons who eat uncontrollably in a hopeless attempt to fill a bottomless hole inside can expect to fail on commercial diets. After all, the *Don't, Don't, Don't* message such diets convey only underscores what the inner-child already knows all too well: I *Can't, Can't, Can't.* Only by getting in touch with *what's eating us* can we gain control over *what we're eating.* With God to help us carry our burdens and pains, it is possible to make the journey to inner healing and physical wellness by facing our fears and gaining control of our food compulsions.

Highlights

- Thinking about food keeps our mind off present concerns and past problems. That's the reward of a food compulsion.
- Long-term effects of uncontrolled eating can be life-threatening. It's better to face pain and deal constructively with it, or to at least work on gaining perspective, than to try eating our problems away.
- God can help us change the *No, No, No* message that underscores our inner-child's doubts and fears, our inner-child's "can't" message, to *Yes, Yes, Yes – Yes, I can!*

Discussion

1. What inner fears might trigger compulsive eating? Why?
2. Why might God be a good source of solace as we fight this problem? How?
3. And how can developing a healthy perspective on the Big Picture – our fears, our inner pain, and our long-term goals – aid the narrower focus of gaining control over what we eat, why we eat, and how we eat . . . just for today?

NINE

Think Wellness!

One young woman phoned me repeatedly from a far southeastern state because she had read one of my books. During our conversation, she expressed so much agitation that I finally said, "You need to discuss those matters with a therapist. Unless at least some of the problems you describe are resolved, you're going to get arthritis."

"Don't talk to me about arthritis," she said. "I have it in every joint of my body, and I'm only 29."

Specific kinds of physical illness are often manifested by clients who come to me with serious psychological problems. I have no medical background, and don't claim medical knowledge. I can only say that clients who come to me for therapy and present a variety of unresolved emotional problems are quite likely to mention that they suffer from such bodily ailments as arthritis, high blood pressure, migraines, gastro-intestinal troubles, and back problems. All too often, they have undergone surgery for cancer, too.

I also have familiarized myself with medical data on bacteria, viruses, and old age. Since bacteria and viruses are always floating around, and since all of us come in contact with them, and since all of us age, it's clear that many factors influence our susceptibility to disease and the effects of aging.

As early as 1958, in fact, L. E. Hinkle and associates were reporting on prime-life-span studies conducted on several groups of people over some 20 years. In this time, scientists found that 25% of group members accounted for 50% of the illnesses, and that another 25% accounted for only 10% of the illnesses. Those persons who suffered the most illness also had a greater number of disease syndromes, both major and minor, involving a greater number of organ systems.

Ah, we think: genes and heredity. Actually, family histories for relatives of the high- and low-illness groups were similar in health and longevity. Both groups, moreover, described similar life-experiences, and both had encountered many difficult life situations. The more frequently ill, however, were more likely to view their lives as difficult, unhappy, and unsatisfactory. Those less frequently ill tended to describe their lives as interesting, varied, and pleasant.

Further, the more frequently ill described their relationships with their parents as "poor," while the less frequently ill viewed their relationships with parents as "good."

The frequently ill tended to be inner-directed and self-absorbed, and keenly aware of emotional problems. The healthier members described little conflict or anxiety in their inter-personal relations, and little awareness of emotional problems.

Increasingly, psychology and medicine are looking at illness and wellness from a more holistic perspective, realizing that a person's health is affected by psychological, spiritual, and social factors as well as by physical conditions. In fact, Dr. E. Shorter of the University of Toronto writes that symptoms of psychosomatic illness are produced not just by an individual's psychology, but also by one's genetic history and even by the time and culture in which we live. "When we fall ill with psychosomatic pain," Shorter says, "our symptoms most often – and quite unconsciously – reflect our particular ethnic group, age, class, or gender." Still, the symptoms and pain are real, and I always refer persons with somatic problems to a physician while, concurrently, providing mental health counseling.

Stress, for instance, plays an important role in one's susceptibility to infectious diseases. Loneliness, especially in persons who have marked dependency needs, may contribute to vulnerability to illness. Similarly, long-term anxiety and long unspoken angers can adversely affect the auto-immune system. And the beliefs and values we hold have an impact on health, as does our self-esteem or lack of it.

How can you and I utilize this knowledge in our lives?

First of all, we must deal with our stress. Writes Dr. Lichtenberg of the University of Kansas, "The stress-illness relationship now seems to be an accepted fact within both psychology and medicine."

I recall two clients in particular, both in their 20s, both too exhausted to work or study, both too tired even to speak clearly. I strained to hear them because they lacked energy enough to project their voices.

One had quit her job as a nurse, and the other had dropped out of a Ph.D. program, too fatigued to continue. As we worked through problems in therapy, each young woman talked about the long-buried angers with which she coped – by forcing them down and out of consciousness. The stress of keeping explosive material buried, however, left both young women without energy to cope with work and study. The remedy was simple: talk out the angers, learn to deal constructively with anger, and, if possible, deal directly with the source of that anger – whoever or whatever it is.

Not all over-stressed persons need therapy, of course. By looking at our lives, each of us can determine our own stress levels. A person, for instance, who is dealing with a sick partner, a load of debt, a business that is expanding and needs a lot of attention, and two young children can determine for him- or herself how to relax and relieve some of the pressure. Perhaps running will do it, maybe mountain-climbing, fishing with friends: Many outlets are available.

Just talking about high-pressure situations, in itself, can offer relief. Social worker Irene Pollin in her 1994 book, *Taking Charge*, tells of experiencing serious stress because of her children's severe illnesses. Yet, because she feared losing control if she talked about her pain, Pollin kept her emotions strictly under cover for several years. Then came a night before her daughter's second open heart surgery; she could no longer restrain herself.

Pollin was attending a symphony with her husband when she was suddenly overcome with a nearly uncontrollable urge to scream. She raced out of the hall, followed by her frightened husband. Only later did the social worker realize she had come within seconds of losing control. Why? Because she had never expressed her stress and anxiety over the next day's surgery.

Never again did she keep her feelings bottled up.

We need, each of us, to look around for ways to relieve stress, discover them, and then incorporate stress relief into our busy schedules.

Modern living bristles with ways in which we can create stress for ourselves: overworking, taking care of everybody, striving to perform perfectly, trying to achieve beyond our ability. God created each of us, and made us as we are. If we can accept that, we can also accept our limitations. Most of us cannot be a perfect wife or model husband, an ideal son or daughter, a genius at studies or work, a saintly priest or religious. God gave us life not to become rich, not to achieve status, but to love God, each other, and ourselves as we are.

And, to expand on a previously noted point, loneliness is a factor here as well. I meet many very lonely clients. Usually, I recommend therapy groups for these people, in addition to personal counseling. Support groups are available for almost any kind of problem and can usually be located through the phone book or by calling your local Catholic Community Services or some other denominational outreach service.

Donna, for instance, suffered extreme loneliness, and was incredibly fearful. She was alienated from her family of origin, and with good reason.

Now, she was attending college but had to work her way through. So she really did not have much time for social activities. Nor would she have trusted anybody enough to make friends if she did have time. Her overwhelming and unreal fears could have been mitigated if only Donna knew more people and enjoyed friends.

It took years for Donna to establish sufficient trust so she could reach out and discover that the world is, on the whole, a pretty good place. But for a deep and sustaining trust in God, she might never have ventured into social relationships. Gradually, she did establish friendships and, consequently, the unreal fears steadily diminished. Her support group was a key to this process. Through their parishes, Catholics and others affiliated with established faith communities, both young and old, can get involved in varied activities and reach out to others who will respond with gratitude. Indeed, even those without a declared faith would be welcome in most churches and synagogues.

Loneliness can be alleviated also by establishing a close relationship with God, the angels, and God's friends in Heaven, too. A woman named Susan Bloom phoned me one day after reading one of my articles and told this wonderful story:

> *My father died a four-years-long death from cancer,* she said. *My mother nursed him throughout. The night before the funeral, I felt very lonesome. I loved him so much.*

Then, during the night, I was awakened by the sound of talking in my room. To my amazement, there stood my father at the foot of my bed, dressed in his old cords and plaid work shirt. He was smiling, sparkling with health, and speaking to a man seated on my bed. I could not see the man's face, but I could see that he wore a lovely white linen robe.

"How will she know we're here?" my father was asking.

"Oh," the younger man replied, "she'll know."

I was speechless with delight — but a nagging small voice told me I must be cracking up; maybe I needed to see a psychiatrist. But I was thrilled. Of course, I was scared, too. And my visitors realized this.

"She's getting frightened," the man told my father. "We'll leave now."

And just like that, they were gone.

After the experience, Susan fell into a happy sleep. Her father had returned, she knew, to let the family know that his time of suffering was ended. Even so, in the morning she wondered, am I going crazy? At first, she told nobody.

But as she sat in a chair waiting for the family to leave for the funeral, she was filled with joy, peace, and a deep happiness. Susan's mother glanced at her. "Whatever happened to you?" the older woman asked. "There's an aura about you."

Then Susan knew it was real, and she shared her good news. Instead of a psychiatrist, she told her pastor. That's real, he said, those things happen. For Susan's family, the nighttime visit relieved both stress and grief.

When we know and believe that our world is peopled with God, the angels, and the saints — including those men, women, and children we love every day — we can feel safe regardless of problems and anxieties. And that sense of security and peace will in turn safeguard our health and protect us from illness.

SUMMARY

While the symtoms and pains of our physical illnesses are very real, they frequently stem from, and mirror, the emotional stresses of our day-to-day lives. Genetics may play a role, but studies have long suggested that attitude is as important as the genes and culture we inherit from our parents in determining how healthy we will be.

Highlights

- Increasingly, psychology and medicine are looking at illness and wellness from a holistic perspective.
- The unhappier we are, the likelier we are to be ill.
- Talking about our problems with others, in itself, can be a big stress reliever.
- Churches, synagogues, and even support groups are places where we might seek out friends. When we have friends, we're less likely to be lonely. And when we're less lonely, we're less likely to be sick.
- If we don't deal with our stress, our problems, our anxieties – we may well increase our chances of getting physically sick.

Discussion

1. How does modern living contribute to the stress in our lives?
2. Why might support groups keep us from getting sick?
3. Does loneliness contribute to illness? Why do you think this might be true?
4. Can prayer help us cope with loneliness? If so, how?
5. What steps can we take in our own lives to minimize stress, anxiety, and loneliness?

TEN

God – Your
No. 1 Stress Buster

Two-thirds of Americans feel stressed at least once every week of their lives, according to a recent poll conducted by Princeton Survey Research Associates. And every one of us, sometime during life, encounters more stress than we can handle. What to do about it?

Eating more broccoli might help, and so might keeping weight down, kicking the cigarette and alcohol habit, exercising faithfully, and getting more than six hours sleep a night. But, says Tom Dybdahl, director of the Stress Prevention Index, Americans do best when they focus on one single behavior change that benefits health and mitigates stress.

The one significant behavior change I suggest is learning a certain kind of trust – a reliance on God and prayer.

God doesn't need me. Not to fulfill God's plans, not to work those eight-hour-days. Not even to race home, cook dinner, and take care of the kids. *I need God.* Everyone *needs* God. And the more stressful life becomes, the *more* everybody *needs* God.

My mother taught me that lesson early in life.

Five years old, I was terrified as a fierce thunder and lightning storm hit the Canadian prairies. It was not unusual for lightning to strike, start a fire, kill an animal or, occasionally, a person. And I saw the lightning hit our windowsill. I screamed for my mother.

"Trust in God, child," came her calm reply.

"But the lightning hit!"

"God takes care of us. Ask God. God won't let the lightning hurt us."

I asked God, relaxed, and the force of the storm moved away.

God holds the whole world close, counts every hair of my head – and yours. God takes care of me – and you.

I can certainly say God has provided for me ever since I prayed that day on the Canadian prairie. God provides for each of us, really. But we do need to ask. We do need to cultivate personal trust in God. Now, many years later, I discover that wisdom anew written in psychological and medical journals, and in health magazines. The outstanding methods of stress reduction, such publications are beginning to tell us with increasing frequency, include religion, meditation, and spirituality.

When we practice our faith we know that God loves and protects us. Safe in God's provident care we can relax, stop gritting our teeth, and learn how to turn stress into an energy gainer instead of an energy wipeout.

For myself, I find immeasurable strength and grace in the daily Eucharist – and I need the guidance and grace because I am a therapist for men and women overwhelmed with stress. And for me, Sunday Mass is a source of grace as well: the Scripture readings, the prayers which encompass our needs and the world's needs, the prayers for peace, the cries for personal forgiveness, and – above all – the reception of the Body and Blood of Jesus in the Eucharistic meal. I *need* Sunday Mass, Scripture, and prayer – if only to deal with my daily stress.

Personally, I need an hour's meditation a day, also, and began that practice when I was 15 years old. I had graduated from high school when I was 14, found myself embroiled in stress at 15, and consequently discovered the refreshing silence of prayer. Regardless of what comes or goes, I've stuck to that daily hour of meditation ever since.

What do I pray about? Well, strangely enough, my hour begins and ends on my mother's favorite prayer: "Sacred Heart of Jesus, I place my trust in Thee."

I learned that prayer from my mother's stories.

When she left Ireland for Canada and marriage to my father, she packed in her trunk her most valued possession: a 17-inch statue of the Sacred Heart. The year was 1914. Her passenger liner was the first chased by a German submarine. All passengers were made aware of near-disaster, but my mother put her faith and trust in the Sacred Heart. She wasn't surprised when her boat outmaneuvered the submarine and all passengers landed safely.

My parents' first home was a log cabin set in a little valley in northern Canada. A lake glistened nearby. In the little cabin, my father had built a small altar for the Sacred Heart statue.

One day my mother glanced out the window to see an approaching prairie fire. "Sacred Heart," she cried, "save my home." Then she ran the mile and a half to the nearest neighbors to warn them, gasped "Fire!" and fainted. Workers from the fields rushed out to plough firebreaks.

That evening my father, a schoolteacher, walked sadly toward the valley to gaze at the ashes of their first little home. But there, standing proud, was the intact log cabin. The fire had approached the cabin, veered in two, raced around it, joined together again and burned madly on until it hit the firebreaks. The Sacred Heart had saved my parents' home.

From the days when, as a small child, I first dusted that statue on Saturday cleaning days, I learned that I could depend on God's providence and the Sacred Heart of Jesus. So it is that daily I spend an hour recalling and leaning on the loving heart of a God Who came to earth to save us. And in that hour I relax.

In varied and sometimes strange ways my clients often describe to me how, in times of severe stress, they discover the benefits of meditation, although they would not recognize that word.

When Margie came to me for psychotherapy, she was grossly overweight, addicted to drink and drugs – growing marijuana in her home, in fact, and severely stressed with conflicts in marriage, her family of origin, and at work. One day, by chance, she opened the huge family Bible – used only to record marriages, births, and deaths – and read a few verses. The words came alive, they brought peace, they sounded wonderful.

Why, she asked herself, had she never read Scripture before? The answer was simple: Her family of origin had no religion. But Scripture opened a whole new world for her. Then and there Margie determined to spend 30 minutes a day reading and pondering the words in that Bible. She had never heard the word, but she was into meditation. As the daily meditation continued, Margie quit drink and drugs – no treatment center or AA. She quit, and never touched them again. Margie lost a hundred pounds, changed jobs and obtained a more suitable position. She also clarified her relationships with her family of origin and subsequently established a happy marriage. The process took three years, and it will require a lifetime to maintain. But Margie and her husband depend upon God for life, love, and a stable marriage now. Their trust, they believe, is well placed.

Margie's therapy with me was important, too. But more important, by far, was her daily meditation and the resultant frequent contact with God. Margie has made several retreats and is always astounded by each new revelation of God. "How could I ever have lived without God?" she wonders now. Margie knows the answer: She did it by drinking, drugging, overeating, over-working madly to keep the stress at bay. Eventually not even addictions could contain the stress. She needed God.

Over and over again I have been amazed by clients whose personal stress was so overpowering that they tried to kill it with drink and drugs, then discovered God, and quit. Just quit.

At this moment I have left a meeting with a new client, a young woman, who related a tale of personal misery, marriage with a man who drank, drugged, and dealt marijuana – which she came to depend on to help *herself* deal with the unbearable stress. Finally he was arrested, she found a church and God, and quit drugs and drink. On her own. With prayer. (She had neither money nor insurance for a treatment center.) "I couldn't go to church and use," she said simply. "I felt like a hypocrite. So I quit." That was five years ago, and she has touched nothing since.

Life in our modern world is seriously stressful. A routine religion alone won't contain the stress. A vibrant, alive, electric consciousness of God is essential.

Several of my clients have found relief from stress, and discovered ways of changing their lives through meditation. They set about this in different ways. Sherry decorated a corner of her bedroom with pictures that appealed to her: Jesus, the ocean, quiet valleys, serene mountain tops. She decided to give herself 30 minutes a day in that corner, all by herself, with no interruptions. (Sherry's day went like this: Get up at 6 a.m.; get breakfast for the children and get them off to school; drive to work; race home to cook dinner for the family, wash dishes and clean up; help the children with homework; collapse into bed and start the next day all over again.)

Teaching her two children, both over 13 at the time, to respect her quiet time in itself took a couple of weeks and resulted in several failed attempts. But Sherry persisted.

And then she found tapes of hymns that refreshed her, and began to play those when she was alone. Gradually, very slowly, Sherry regained control of her life.

When Sherry first came to see me, she was suffering pain in all of her joints. Doctors never did find out what ailed her. But it doesn't matter anymore. Because now, several years later, Sherry is pain free. And she loves her daily quiet time alone.

For his part, Bob found relief from stress in his rosary.

His family had no religion, and was in fact anti-religious. But, when he was eight years old, both of Bob's parents obtained work in a Catholic hospital.

"We'll take this little boy into our school tuition-free," the Sister running the hospital said.

Bob had only one year in that Catholic school, but he learned about God and prayer in that time, slipped into Mass every day, and learned the rosary. Bob is a young man now, and until this past year his life has been one of hard work and misery. He has survived incredible stress without major psychological damage.

"How did you do it?" I asked him once.

"I prayed my rosary every night before I went to sleep," he answered simply. "It calmed me down. The rosary and my one year in a Catholic school saved my sanity and my life."

The rosary can be a valuable stress-reducer. Prayerful repetition of the same words, over and over, is soothing to a mind that has raced throughout the day. I have another client who belongs to a rosary group and never – regardless of pressures, and they are many – misses her time with the rosary.

The POWs who endured the Hanoi Hilton all attributed their survival to sheer grace and a growing closeness to God and each other. In the final analysis, life is what we make it. Within our own souls God has placed the resources to cope effectively with stress. We need only discover our inner resources and use them. To obtain the grace that can sustain us through tough times, we need to pray.

Occasionally, we need the assistance as well of mental health experts to help us unlock the strengths with which God gifted us. Pearl, for instance, took care of everybody. In particular, she took care of her mother. She came to me because of severe stress.

Pearl's memory of her last day in her home is painful. She lay on the bed with both parents beating her so hard that she feared they would break her back. Nevertheless, after Pearl graduated from college – she worked her way through – she got married and took her parents with her on her honeymoon.

"Pearl," I asked, "how could you?"

"Well, they said I should," she told me, "and I'm obedient."

Pearl went on to get her Ph.D. When first she came to me, she taught in a community college, and had undergone cancer surgery. And I discovered that Pearl was all the while sending cards and gifts to her siblings for Christmas and their birthdays, no matter how sick she was. Of course, she was sending gifts to her mother, too.

"Do any of them send cards and gifts to you?" I questioned.

"No."

"Then why send them to your siblings? They're grown and have their own families."

"Well, I have to take care of them. Somebody has to."

It turned out that Pearl had practically raised her brothers and sisters. Forgetting that they are grown, she was continuing to parent them. It was only with difficulty that Pearl abandoned parenting her brothers and sisters. Why? Because she had carried on with the practice for so long. Had they reciprocated, her cards and gifts would have made sense. But Pearl's family took her consideration for granted.

Then I learned that Pearl's mother regularly came to Pearl's own home for Christmas and Thanksgiving. But, regardless of how hard Pearl worked to pull off a perfect day, her mother started such an unbearable argument – mainly by downgrading Pearl at the festive dinner – that Pearl was always left in tears. "Don't invite your mother," I suggested.

But Pearl *had* to invite her mother. That sort of thing, she told me, is required by the Fourth Commandment. I assured her, however, that the Fourth Commandment reqires parents to love and care for their children in turn. When they have failed their half of the Commandment – rather spectacularly in Pearl's case – our continued duty is no longer mandated. (By this time, Pearl was undergoing a second surgery for cancer.)

It was obvious to me that Pearl was under severe emotional stress. She phoned and wrote her mother regularly, and made trips to ensure that the older woman was properly cared for. When I asked Pearl to detach from her mother, the young woman wept.

"But," she cried, "who will take care of her?" (Pearl's father had died some years before.) I assured Pearl that her mother was skilled in getting whatever help she needed and could certainly manage on her own. Finally, Pearl agreed. Pearl's husband, meantime, would maintain contact with the mother if necessary.

Pearl gradually recovered from stress. Gradually means over several months. By degrees, Pearl began to win back her health. One year later she checked on her mother: By now, the woman had a variety of volunteers from church taking care of her, and a younger man had just proposed marriage. She had never needed Pearl.

It's easy to fall into the "taking-care-of-everybody-but-me" mode. But it's seriously stressful. And it does neither "everybody" nor "me" any good.

God gave each of us the ability to take care of ourselves. If we have not learned how, then we had best ask God to teach us.

Stress is a serious and pervasive American problem. The more we advance in high technology, in speed and efficiency, the more likely we are to find ourselves out of touch with life's bare essentials, and the more stressful life is likely to be become. But we can bring our stress to God and thus overcome it. God can take us back to basics. Stress, then, can be most effectively countered with religion, meditation, spirituality, and prayer.

SUMMARY

Stress affects every one of us. In looking for stress busters, ways to beat stress, we're most likely to find answers in God and prayer. Many people, for instance, find meditative prayer to be quite effective in refocusing their perspective on what's really important. And so prayer, in all its forms and styles – along with learning to set healthy limits – may well be the answer to your search for stress relief.

Highlights

- In addition to daily meditative prayer, spiritual reading (Scripture or some other insightful tracts), saying the rosary, and making retreats can all help us fight stress.

- Finding a suitable place for prayer is just as important as prayer itself, for without a *place* to pray, we probably can't pray, even if we want to pray.
- Music, particularly spiritual classics, can help us relax.

Discussion

1. Why must our fight against stress be vibrant, alive, and electric in our consciousness of God?

2. What kinds of stress do you have in your life? How do these stressors keep you "off center" at times?

3. What kinds of prayer do you think might be effective in your fight against stress? Why? How and where might you find opportunity to pray?

ELEVEN

I Can't Cope!

Finally, after a tough week at work, you've found a spare Saturday moment to water the lawn. You drag out the garden hose. Congratulating yourself for being the can-do type you've always wanted to be, you turn to the faucet and give it a turn.

The spigot creaks open. You hear the sound of water gurgling through rubber tubing and bend over to pick up the nozzle. *SHHH-squirt-t-t!*

The wet blast to your backside is exactly what you were afraid of – the hose coupling has finally loosed its tenuous grasp from the handy hose-caddy. Water is squirting everywhere, including all over you. The dog, appearing to have more common sense, beats a hasty retreat to the backyard.

Well, that's life. Or so you tell yourself, feeling a little smug for having kept your cool. With a deliberate motion, you pick up the coupling and try to screw it all back together. Too late you realize dry rot has gotten to the hose; it'll have to be repaired before any lawn watering can occur. So you leap up the porch steps two at a time, dash into the kitchen, and grab the car keys off their designated peg. Without a second thought, you and the dog hop into your aging roadster and chug off to the hardware store.

While there, you figure: Why not? Let's kill three birds with one stone.

So you pick up a couple of bags of lawn patch. With your free arm you snag a box of fertilizer. If you're going to work on lawn and garden today, you might as well do things right. As you head for the checkout counter the little lightbulb of remembrance flickers.

"Aha!" you mutter. "Almost forgot the hose coupling!"

But the good news is, you did not! Chuckling to yourself, you head once more for the checkout line. It's going to be a good day after all.

With a sigh of relief, you heave your burdens onto the counter. (Lawn patch seems heavier this year than it did last, but never mind.) As you return the cashier's friendly hello, you reach toward your back pocket. And even as your hand moves toward your backside you find your patience being challenged all over again.

No wallet.

Some days, you wonder if a new day dawns just to taunt you. But it isn't until you return home that you realize you left your wallet in the glove box of your car the other day. For sure: it was right where you needed it all along.

To your credit, you do not grit your teeth. In fact, it's not until you notice the dog digging up the freshly planted petunias that you really lose it. Only then do you fight back the urge to scream primeval: *"Daggnabbit! I can't cope!"*

Ever notice how the little things are the ones that really get us going?

Well, that's what we tell ourselves. But if we find ourselves losing our tempers again and yet again, something's wrong. It's time to take stock of our lives.

What needs changing?

What is left undone? What needs attention?

What's eating us, anyway?

Times come in our lives when we need to make changes. Sometimes, in fact, major changes are called for. Should we find ourselves in such a place, a visit to a professional therapist may be the best option; we may need to develop a plan to turn our lives around.

More often than not, though, it's the little things that build up until we feel we just can't take it anymore. The day-to-day rigors: cleaning the house or the apartment; doing the laundry week after week; driving the kids here, there, and everywhere; doing the mending; washing the dishes; mowing the lawn; mediating squabbles; keeping groceries in the fridge; volunteering with the block club; helping with calculus homework; keeping the career on track; keeping the boss off our back; keeping up with the Joneses. Whew!

Where does it all end? The truth is, it ends with us. When life crowds in and we think we just can't take it anymore, even if a major change isn't called for, we ought to pay attention. Too many things left undone – even if it's *ourselves* that we're neglecting – will catch up to us. When all the little things seem out of control, we must take a closer look within.

Here's How

Put the Situation in Perspective.

Mary felt depressed. The president of her growing and successful company had just asked her to become his personal assistant. He had added offices to the space he already owned. He wanted Mary to move into the front office to meet clients – to greet clients with him, to take conference phone calls with him.

And so he introduced her to her new office: three sides were encased in glass and revealed breathtaking views of mountains and the Pacific Ocean.

But the move, Mary knew, would take her out of the cozy atmosphere of the space she shared with other office workers. And so Mary found herself at her desk, ready to cry. What if this move was really happening because the others had complained about her? What if they really didn't like her? Was the president moving her to a space where she wouldn't bother anybody else?

Common sense, of course, told Mary otherwise. Nevertheless, she couldn't feel peaceful about her promotion until she had talked the problem over with two of her assistants. They, of course, understood and helped her put the situation in perspective. In fact, the situation was just the opposite of her fears: She got along with office personnel *so well* that now the president wanted her to represent the company to business persons who arrived to make deals that were crucial to the company's welfare, to welcome them in her usual pleasant manner and play a key role in drumming up new business.

Count Your Blessings.

Rebecca's work as a consultant required her to make public presentations. But Rebecca had always been a person with great fears. She recalled lying in her bed at three or four years of age, trying to mask all signs of her own breathing. If somebody came to kill her, Rebecca figured, the intruder wouldn't know she was there.

"I was so scared . . ." she told me. "Always so scared. In my childish innocence, I figured that invisible evil was going to kill me."

Not surprisingly, the 33-year-old woman's childhood years were distorted by violence and abuse.

Finally, Rebecca confessed her fears to a friend. "If only I had something to hang on to," she said, "it would help a lot. I'm just so terrified of making public presentations."

"Well," her friend responded, "I'm getting a new rosary. You can have this one."

"I put that rosary in my pocket," said Rebecca. "Now when I'm presenting to a big group, I clutch it, hard. It made me feel like I had a little bit of God in my pocket, even though I didn't know any of the prayers."

One day, when she felt more ill-at-ease than usual, Rebecca, with a couple of friends, dropped in at a local church. Suddenly she felt at home. "I knew evil couldn't get me there. At last, I'd found a spot that provided sanctuary . . . and safety . . . and peace."

Rebecca began attending Mass; she learned to say the rosary, and she discovered holy water. Gradually, through the Eucharist, the rosary, baptism, and the gift of holy water, Rebecca found peace and release from the wordless fears that had clouded her young life from her earliest days. She had, literally, learned to count the blessings which God had provided in abundance to keep her safe.

Call a Friend.

One client tends to suffer from intermittent depression. Even when nothing in particular goes wrong, she allows herself to dwell on a painful past and ends up in the dumps. But this woman is the kind of person who has made many friends along her life's path. And along the way, she has learned to phone a friend and enjoy a chat – even if it's about nothing in particular. For her, that's a liberating experience.

I note similar positive effects most particularly with clients who belong to AA: They always have friends to call, persons who will help in a constructive manner, and who won't hesitate to point out the problem between the client and his or her doom and gloom nightshade.

One suggestion, though: Don't always call the same friend; it's not fair to dump exclusively on one other person.

Treat Yourself to Something Special.

I write this with a bit of apprehension because, too often, the "something special" is candy, cake, or ice cream. And giving yourself that kind of treat is usually not smart because the long-term effect of sugar is depression – and that will only leave you feeling less able to cope than before. To guzzle candy because we're depressed or feeling out of control offers momentary relief but, in the long run, increases our chances of feeling negative emotions.

One client, for instance, quit a life of prostitution which she had always hated. Next, she gave up drugs and alcohol – needed formerly to deaden her feelings.

Now, she needed education to prepare herself for employment and also came to me for therapy. She had made several momentous life changes in the space of a couple of weeks. Yet, overwhelmed by the need for *something*, she turned to ice cream, occasionally eating an entire gallon at once. Of course she began putting on weight, and soon fell into a depression. I guided her to understand the alternatives to food by which we can help ourselves cope.

A multitude of something specials that do no harm, on the other hand, *can* be found: Go to a movie, investigate a few thrift shops for bargains, drive to one of your city's lovely viewpoints, plan your next vacation, take the dog for a run, give the cat extra affection and get loads of it back, enjoy a brisk walk, go to the library for a book, tape, or video, locate a swimming pool and enjoy.

Say a Prayer.

I especially recommend St. Anthony of Padua and St. Jude. The first is noted for finding lost objects, and the second for aiding hopeless cases. Both saints have helped so many people, so well, that recent books have appeared about them.(I might mention that when I visited Padua, Italy, last summer our tour guide said that young women in Italy pray to St. Anthony for a husband! "And," she added, "they always get a good one!")

Take a Walk.

A good fast walk is a restorative. Further, a brisk walk motivates our brains to release endorphins which have a tranquilizing effect on us. A walk can make us feel better physically, and often spiritually too.

Do Something Special for Somebody Who is Worse Off.

An effort to help others can take our minds off our own problems, which may actually seem miniscule in proportion to the pain of others.

One client in therapy with me also attended group therapy. When a member of the group had to undergo brain surgery and was forced to return to work too early because she had no other means of income, my client volunteered to pay the cost of group therapy for the sick woman. Her anonymous action benefited the sick person, but my client also helped herself. Realizing that she has a good husband, a wonderful home, and a satisfying work environment enabled my client to count blessings she had not previously recognized.

And I myself recall the hundreds of St. Vincent de Paul calls I've made through the years, and how sincerely I came to appreciate a decent dwelling with adequate food and sleep as a result. Many of us fail to realize how well off we really are.

Accept the Things You Cannot Change.

Perhaps we grew up in an unhealthy environment. "I was forced to learn at a very young age to swallow my feelings," one client wrote. "Never allow anger to show. I learned at that early age that it was neither safe nor acceptable to *feel*. I learned to *act* like everything was OK. Throughout the abuse of my early years I learned not to trust. I believed the big people in my life who told me that I was worthless and would never amount to anything. As a result I don't know how to have a healthy intimate relationship."

Once this man, Ray, realized and accepted those painful facts, however, instead of denying and repressing them, he was able to work through the pain in therapy and to develop the talents and brilliance and communications skills he'd always had.

He'd kept these things hidden because, as a child, he had learned to hide *everything*.

We can't change our childhoods. But until we accept situations as they are, we can't work through the damaging effects of early childhood abuse, or whatever problem may beset us.

We need to accept facts about ourselves, too: Perhaps we're too smart or too dumb; maybe our feet are too big or our noses too small; maybe we're physically weak and don't cope as well as other people. Fighting the facts of life uses up energy, leaves us without resources for everyday living, and doesn't change a thing.

Talk to Yourself, Kindly.

We're often our own worst enemies. We routinely toss cutting words at ourselves. But we *can* learn, slowly and gradually, to compliment ourselves with words that provide nourishment: *"I'm a good person . . . God loves me . . . I handled such-and-such well . . . I have a guardian angel to watch over me . . . I do try to help others . . ."*

I encourage my clients to give themselves positive reinforcement whenever possible. Life *is* challenging, and we need all the help we can get.

Listen to a Favorite Song.

Thousands of lonesome Irish immigrants cheered themselves with *Danny Boy, The Wearin' of the Green,* and *Killarney.* And immigrants from other countries carry their own native songs in their hearts, also, as they come to America. We can choose from hundreds of catchy songs taken, for instance, from musicals such as *The Sound of Music,* or from traditional hymns that touch us. Even catchy tunes from a rock band can do the trick. Listening to a tape or singing to ourselves can certainly change our mood when life momentarily turns sour.

Enjoy Some Quiet Time All by Yourself.

Life in these United States seems to go ever faster, almost as if it's trapping us in some kind of perpetual motion machine. Taking half an hour of quiet time may seem selfish, but it might also be essential to our sanity. My clients routinely accuse themselves of selfishness where there is none. Once, for example, I asked members of a group therapy session to do something just for themselves. Came a chorus of dissent: *"Oh, I do so much for myself as it is, I'd be embarrassed . . . I always take care of myself . . . I take more care of me than of my family . . ."*

Nevertheless, I insisted: Just do *one* thing only for you and let me hear next week what that was.

At the next session, several faces were red with embarrassment: One person bought herself a pair of jeans for $12; one read a book for a half-hour while her husband got ready for bed; one managed to look through a magazine; one went into a store to purchase an item for herself and found that she could not, though she had money enough; one burst into tears and finally explained she had not been able to do anything for herself even though she tried.

And so I encourage you, too, dear reader, to try giving yourself a half-hour of quiet time alone daily, just to enjoy.

Make Amends If Necessary.

Nothing gets us down like guilt – and I mean real guilt from a real misdeed. (Many persons are plagued with overall feelings of guilt which are not based on reality, but are neurotic.) If, however, I've lied to someone, or stolen an item of value, or cheated – the list goes on, and we know ourselves what specific action was wrong – then for the sake of our own peace of mind, not to mention our peace with God, we ought to admit the misdeed and make amends.

If we've shoplifted, for instance, we can remit the money to the store with a cashier's check. If we've lied to a neighbor, we can tell the truth. If we've cheated on taxes, we can discuss the remedy with an accountant. The effort to march on and keep smiling when we're nagged by a dozen guilts uses up more energy than we have at our disposal. The end of the matter is fatigue – and then the I-Can't-Cope Syndrome.

Face the Possibility of Failure.

Failure is not the end of life. Nobody succeeds all the time. We can't always win.

If we face the future with the realistic estimate of some failures factored in, we do ourselves a favor. Besides, failure may open the door to a greater reward.

On one occasion I lost a job I enjoyed. I felt terrible. But then my superiors asked me to write a book. The result of that book, and the one after that, was the start of Shepherd's Counseling Services ten years ago, an organization I founded to provide psychotherapy to those who otherwise could not afford it. Now, we have seven therapists, an active Board of Directors, and hundreds of clients, both women and men, whom we serve on a sliding-fee basis. Since starting Shepherd's Associates, I've appeared on almost 200 TV and radio shows with messages that, I hope, have helped listeners. And I've consequently received hundreds of letters.

One of my clients who lost a position he valued was very despondent. In his free time, though, he started designing and painting. Now, three years later, his canvases sell for $50,000 each.

God knows best. We may never figure out God's overall purpose, but my experience shows clearly that one door never closes without God's interest and love opening the next on life's journey.

Make One Small Permanent Change.

During the black periods when we feel hopeless, we can always look for one change we've long wanted to make but never had the time . . . or the courage. Jim, for instance, realized that never in his life had he taken a vacation, never learned how to ski, never watched a hockey game, never traveled to a different city, never did anything fun.

So he set out to remedy that – though he did need supportive therapy to do so because his early life had been one of severe deprivation. Maybe the only change we make is adopting a new hairstyle, or winning a new friend, or taking weekly adventure in the public library or surfing the Internet. The effort to instill a small change will channel thoughts away from I-Can't-Cope helplessness.

Finally, God's in heaven, and all's right with the world because, regardless of how bad situations appear at any given moment, God's Providence inevitably draws good out of evil. In the long run, good will triumph. Nothing could have been worse than death by crucifixion, but God followed through with an offer of Resurrection and new life.

SUMMARY

When we're at our wits end, it's time to take stock. Is it the little things that are getting to us – or is there some bigger, deeper problem that's bugging us? If necessary, a therapist can help us make this determination. Otherwise, we can make a smaller change, help others less fortunate than ourselves, or listen to a good musical score and unwind a little.

Highlights

- Depression can set in if we're stressed for too long with too little support.
- Friends, life's little blessings, quiet time, and a healthy perspective – all can help us cope when things get tough.
- Struggling to balance our responsibilities is normal. Indeed, it is not selfish to be kind to ourselves and treat ourselves to a harmless little pleasure when we're feeling unglued.

Discussion

1. Have you ever had trouble coping? How?
2. How did you resolve the situation? Did any of the suggestions in this chapter give you an idea of how you might have handled the situation differently? Which one?
3. Which coping tip do you like best? Why? Can you see yourself implementing this into your own lifestyle? How?

TWELVE

When I Take Care of Everybody But Me

Almost every person who comes to Shepherd's Counseling Services for therapy is taking care of everybody but her- or himself. That behavior appears to spring from the child's taking on an early burden of responsibility for the happiness of parents and, usually, of siblings as well. Almost all my clients attained adulthood in seriously dysfunctional families.

When, for instance, I asked Jill to describe her parents to me, the only early image of her mother she could visualize was of a threatening woman holding knives. Her father had abused Jill for years. Nevertheless, she visited her parents regularly and took care of them in a variety of ways.

Jeri came to me in her 40s. I discovered she regularly sent flowers to her mother, phoned her daily, mailed cards and gifts. All this in spite of the fact that her mother had abused Jeri physically, emotionally, and sexually throughout childhood and the teen years. But Jeri's job, as a child, was to make her mother happy, and she was deeply committed to that job. Only slowly, gradually was she able to relinquish it and accept her most basic need: self-care.

Ron was both mother and father to his siblings. Ron's own father was often gone, and his mother was a drug and alcohol addict. So from an early age, Ron cooked for his brothers and sisters, cleaned the house, and made money for the family. In his sophomore year, in fact, he quit school so he could work and make money to give to his parents. Indeed, he never stopped working; right up to the time he first saw me, Ron continued to *overwork*. And even for some years afterward, he kept up the pace.

As a matter of fact, Ron is struggling to recover from pneumonia right now. He has been hospitalized, is confined to bed with a temperature, and is generally rundown. But Ron is not an old man. He is a very *young* man. His physical resources, though, have been seriously undermined by years and years of overwork.

In their early years abused children are so often accused of laziness and selfishness that they internalize the message. Changing the old tapes takes time and requires deep trust in a therapist before a client can relinquish the ancient, life-long messages of inadequacy.

Jean is a social worker with a good position. When she first initiated therapy with me, Jean was living at home with her mother and father. One day, she complained that her mother opened and read all her mail. "Why don't you move out?" I queried. "You're getting a good salary and certainly can afford to."

By staying at home, Jean explained, she could pay rent to her parents and help them out in that way.

Were they in need of the money?

"Well, no," Jean answered. "But they said I should." In subsequent sessions, Jean continued to relate serious invasions of privacy – not to mention incidents of abuse from both parents through childhood. Eventually, with therapy, Jean worked up the courage to move out. She did, however, leave one small box of clothing with her mother because her Volkswagon bug couldn't hold more.

That Christmas Jean got a present in the mail from her mother. Very excited – this would be her first gift – she tore open the wrapping. The parcel contained a pair of her own old shoes, left behind in the small box of clothing.

Persons who take care of everybody but themselves need to change or die young. Why? As they mature, they inevitably take care of everybody they come across: work colleagues, friends, partners – whomever. Often they take care of their work supervisor, training in new employees for the "boss," completing any work left over at quitting time, being super-watchful that all goes well for the supervisor – who is given the place once reserved for the mother or father long ago.

Even so, each client who works the painful way out of taking care of the world feels guilty, feels selfish. I remind each that when Jesus gave us the two greatest commandments, he said that the first is to love God above all things. The second is to love our neighbors as *ourselves*.

As ourselves. God made us, and God made us good. We are created in God's image and likeness. We are, each of us, created *good persons*, and therefore it's all right to love ourselves, take proper care of our health, and develop our intellectual capacities.

Self-improvement is not laziness, nor is it selfish. Self-care and authentic self-love show reverence for that very special creation of God – us.

Kitty certainly managed to take care of everybody but Kitty in a spectacular manner. A Native American, Kitty had managed to raise a child while a single parent with no child support; she also went to college and became a registered nurse. In that time, she quit drinking, addressing her own alcoholism without support from a treatment center or AA. She lacked money for the first, she told me, and time for the second.

Kitty's childhood had been abusive, full of beatings and physical pain. Throughout life she had worked long hard hours without ever taking time off, and had cared adequately for her child who was now a happily married adult. After three months of therapy, Kitty said she was tired, so tired that she could hardly keep going. By this point, she was married and caring for two step-children and their father, her husband. I suggested she take time for the rest needed.

Kitty took me literally. She went to bed. Period. She came regularly to therapy, and ate when she woke up. Beyond that, she slept pretty much 24 hours a day. This continued week after week. It sounded a bit extreme, so I finally inquired whether she might be taking sleeping pills? No. Any other medication? Nothing.

A lifetime of stress and strain had taken its toll, and now, obviously, her physical system demanded time to recuperate. Nevertheless, I had never experienced a client who took care of herself this dramatically.

Eventually Kitty obtained enough sleep. Then she threw herself energetically into life again, but this time with self-care factored in.

This year, Kitty's Christmas card to me carried a significant message: "I'm working as a Public Health Nurse for my Tribe," she wrote. "And, starting in 1996, I'll be director of the AIDS program for the Reservation and the County. I was selected to sit on the state HIV Prevention Planning Council (beat out 46 applicants). I'm busy all the time, and both of the above committees require travel."

When we give ourselves adequate care, we do *more* with greater efficiency.

The Steps to Wholeness

Understanding Self-esteem.

Self-esteem, an appreciation of myself, is rooted in the fact that God made me, and God made me good. God expects me to take care of myself, to develop my talents, and to reach out for at least a reasonable degree of happiness.

Understanding Childhood's Contribution to Self-esteem.

During their most formative years children should be treated as valuable and important persons. They should be protected from violence – physical, emotional, and sexual – so they might develop in an atmosphere conducive to self-confidence.

The family needs to set rules and boundaries for the child along with a supportive structure, so the child is able to distinguish between his or her own life and that of other family members.

Children need to have work: schoolwork or household chores, through the execution of which they are validated and appreciated. This fosters the development of self-confidence along with a sense of security and orderliness in the world as a whole.

Children learn there is no one specific solution to the problems of life when they are encouraged to experiment and try out the new as opposed to the old.

The ability, as an adult, to innovate and take self-responsibility is dependent on a childhood that promoted self-esteem and self-trust by reason of stability and continuity at the family base.

What If None of the Above Applies?

Persons who realize, from the above description, that their own childhood was not nourishing – remember, too, that *none* of us had a completely functional family – that their own childhood nurture was lacking to an extreme degree, may have become caretakers. If so, they need to break free of the early childhood conditioning and develop a new self-appreciation.

Keep in mind here that self-esteem is not infrequently sought by methods that don't work: popularity, prestige, money and what money can buy, or sexual conquests. We can strive to belong to the right clubs, or the right political factions, or the right religion. We can maintain loyalty to groups that are destructive, and try to purchase appreciation by giving expensive gifts. We can fool ourselves endlessly in the effort to promote others' opinions of ourselves, hoping thus to gain self-esteem. But that exterior facade of self-esteem won't last, and is not, in any case, helpful. Self-esteem is based on my inner reality and conviction. It's based on what I think and feel about me, not on what others express.

Authentic self-regard, if not established during childhood and nourished throughout our growing years, is best developed later in life by meditation on the fact that God made us, and God made us good. Because we are God's precious creation, each of us, we have cause to value ourselves. Each of us is unique, and therefore we have a right to develop those specific gifts God gave us. Certainly, we must be very important persons because God's only Son took on our flesh to redeem and save us through a horrible death – and then rose again: Redeemer and God!

SUMMARY

Taking care of everybody but ourselves is a way of life we adopt when our childhood was damaged in a very specific way. In short, we did not receive an affirming upbringing with sufficient guidance and nurture from the significant adults in our lives. As a result, we lack the skills we need to set clear boundaries, examine our own needs, meet our own needs, or ask for help in doing so.

Highlights

- When we take care of everybody but ourselves, we neglect ourselves to our own emotional and physical peril.
- Wanting good health and wanting a healthy academic and social life are not selfish wants. These are reasonable and healthy desires.

- It is not wrong to love ourselves. After all, God loves us and wants the best for us.

Discussion

1. Do you frequently take care of everybody but you?

2. Did you relate to any of the scenarios in this chapter? Which ones? In what ways?

3. Has taking care of others ever caused you to experience negative consequences or pain? What kind? When?

4. What steps can you take now to break the pattern in your life of taking care of everybody but you? Write them down.

THIRTEEN

How to Live with a Teenager

Teenagers want to be challenged. For 30 years I was a high school principal of teenage girls, most of whom were adjudicated delinquent and sent to our Good Shepherd schools by juvenile courts. In fact, most of these adolescents had run away from home because of physical and/or sexual abuse, were too young to provide for their own basic needs, and consequently committed illegal acts. Others were simply neglected.

In this context I worked individually with at least 3,000 adolescent girls. These were troubled youngsters. And the first time a teenager said to me: "I know you really love me. Can you guess why?" I stood there without an answer.

But it was a statement repeated numerous times.

Always, the answers were along similar lines. "Because," the youth would say, "when I did such-and-such wrong, you corrected me. It would have been much easier for you to let me slide. But you never did."

That's right. Time after time, these young people said the same thing: "You took the trouble to point out my problems. That's how I knew you really cared."

I was amazed. But in the process I learned a basic fact: Teens don't want to just get by. They want, and need, an adult who will say, clearly, "Your behavior is unacceptable" when, in fact, that's the case.

Young people also want adults to believe in them, tell them they can succeed. Nobody proved this to me quite like Ann Marie.

Our Good Shepherd schools accepted only teens of average intelligence, or higher. Ann Marie's I.Q. score, however, was much lower – in the 60s. Still, I felt certain the young woman did indeed possess average intelligence, and so I endeavored to develop her self-confidence. Over and over I assured her that she was as capable as her classmates, and urged her to study.

But I was the only person who believed in Ann Marie: One day a social worker came to our school and took Ann Marie away. A state school for mentally handicapped adolescents, the social worker believed, was the proper place for Ann Marie.

I wept bitter tears. Would Ann Marie's budding self-confidence be forever frozen? I decided to pray the Litany of Our Lady for the teenager every night. And I continued to do so for 25 years.

It would be that long before I learned Ann Marie's fate. That's when I visited the city in which she lived. But I didn't know that. I found out because Ann Marie came to see me. Now, she was a practical nurse. She had believed me! Because of my belief in her potential, Ann Marie told me, *she* had believed in herself. And that's why she succeeded.

Even more than affirmation, though, teenagers need adults whom they trust enough to talk to. But most parents today don't have much time available to nurture the bonds and give teens the space they need. I do, however, know one married couple who is the exception, and I count them among my best friends. Both are executives, and I've known them for years.

Both work full time at demanding professions, and have done so ever since their second child was four. Even so, they consistently give quality time to both children. Six nights a week dinner is eaten together. Through the children's teenage years, the first priority after business trips for this couple always was spending time with the children. Consequently, both children are well adjusted. Thus, I know that parents can work at time-consuming jobs and still give teens the time and attention they need.

By contrast, most youth sent to our Good Shepherd schools possessed poor interpersonal skills. They tended to be socially ineffective with adults, and were less likely to defer to adult authority. Usually their problems had developed in a dysfunctional home atmosphere where parents were more likely to give commands to their children, to reward deviant behavior by giving it more attention, and to ignore socialized behavior.

But teenagers don't enjoy living this way, and they don't thrive when raised this way. In my years at the Good Shepherd School, we Sisters, the important adults in their lives, taught socialization to these troubled young women and modeled it, offered corrective feedback, praised socially acceptable behavior, and made ourselves emotionally available to them. Always with children, consistent modeling is of primary importance; and so is spending structured time with adults important for youth. That's why it's essential that parents make time for their teenagers and, by example, teach them how to act in social and interpersonal situations.

I doubt, in fact, that any plan beats the family dinner shared together. Not all parents can realistically do this, of course. Single parents have a particularly difficult problem in setting aside special time for teens. Nevertheless, teenagers urgently need to spend quality time with healthy adults.

Those who suffer the lack turn to peer groups in seeking to get needs met. In inner cities, such groups tend to be gangs. And so, if teenagers don't have two parents who can give them support and a listening ear, they need alternative adults: relatives, coaches, counselors, Big Brothers or Sisters.

In my work with Seattle's United Indians of All Tribes, I notice children's needs being met in innovative ways. When one young physically handicapped woman's hyperactive child became unmanageable, for instance, she called the agency for crisis assistance.

The agency responded by sending a Kia, an Indian grandmother, to the family. Though neither mother nor son is Indian, Kia gladly takes the child on outings and keeps him busy. She is available to the mother as well, who phones and chats with her "grandmother" often.

For every difficulty, then, an answer can be found. But such answers must be searched out.

Exercise is a priority for teenagers, too. Why? Currently too many teenagers spend evenings in front of the TV and while they watch TV, they eat snacks. As a result, they gain weight.

Most schools today offer many activities, but most teens need encouragement to become involved. They need parents who spend at least some time watching their competitive games. Again, time is a factor for busy parents. Particularly busy parents, however, might coach soccer or baseball, and in so doing get exercise themselves.

And teenagers need clothes, lots of them. Catholic schools usually require uniforms which save time and money for parents, as well as take the edge off teenagers' obsession with the latest styles. Indeed, a few public schools now require uniforms as well – if only to cut down on theft and worse; in some schools stabbings have resulted over a victim's expensive team jacket or athletic shoes.

When budgets are tight, I suggest taking a shrewd look in thrift shops.

Teenagers need religion as well. I say this because most troubled adolescents sent to Good Shepherd schools knew little about God, and less about prayer. Usually, however, they were attracted to our religious atmosphere, and asked many questions. Though they could be baptized or join the Catholic church only with parental consent, this consent was usually obtained without difficulty since the youths' parents often had no religion themselves.

Why is religion so important? Religion does more for us than give us a forum for prayer – much more. Often, religion offers us a sound set of common-sense rules for everyday living, in our community and in our culture. And our passing these messages of moderation and self-control on to our children is probably the best gift we'll ever give them.

Life poses many choices, and showing kids how – with the help of a religious code – to make good choices in life is a mighty task indeed. Religion, of course, helps parents do that.

More than anything, though, teenagers want adults who care enough to teach them how to relate and contribute to society; adults who challenge them; adults who help fulfill their needs in acceptable ways; adults who give them time and personal attention.

And in no small way, faith figures into this equation. Teens want adults to offer them a religious faith for those moments when life requires something more. And that faith must be strong enough to provide young people with a stable support as they weather the troubling storms of life.

SUMMARY

Young people often perform according to our expectations. If we expect nothing, that may well be what we get. If we expect great things – well, they just might impress us accordingly. In particular, a strong support network of adults who listen, advise, and offer appropriate social modeling is crucial in helping young people grow into well-adjusted adults. Our young people need religion, too. If we give it to them, they'll be prepared when life throws them a moral curve.

Highlights

- A young person's life can be changed by one adult who simply *believes* in that teenager.

- Teenagers need adults who listen well and fulfill their needs in other acceptable ways.

- Young people need clear boundaries in life, and they need adults around them who will establish and maintain these boundaries, or limits.

- Teenagers will do what they need to do to get attention, including engaging in negative behaviors. So it's best to affirm and reinforce the good things they do as soon as we see these positive behaviors occur.

Discussion

1. What kinds of problems do single parents, in particular, face? How do these problems differ from two-parent households? How can a single parent meet these added challenges?

2. Why do young people need an understanding of virtues in their lives?

3. What are some ways we can challenge the young people we love? In what ways can we add structure to their lives? Why are these things important?

FOURTEEN

How to Keep Your Marriage Happy

John and Lois Kloeck act like newlyweds: They shoot shy glances in one another's direction; they hold hands; they quickly defer to one another. They are, obviously, in love.

Yet John and Lois have been married for 58 years. And, clearly, they are more in love today than when they married.

Since John is a conservative Catholic, though, I found one thing perplexing. "How," I asked him, "could you have allowed yourself to fall in love with a Protestant woman?" Back in those rigid days, mixed marriages took place in the rectory, not in the church. Knowing John's deep, sustaining faith, I couldn't imagine him courting a person whose religion differed from his. At my question, he shot a quick, loving glance at Lois.

"How could I *not* have married her?" he exclaimed. "I couldn't help it. I asked her, and she said yes."

A genuine love for each other, apart from a mutual sexual attraction, is mandatory before marriage takes place. Then, with that kind of 20-karat burnished love setting the stage, partners can withstand the friction and conflict inescapable when two persons make a life-long commitment to each other.

"Judy and I married when both of us were still in college," says another friend of mine, Chuck Barnes. "I was 21 and she was 20. It was a dumb thing to do at the time. I looked at Judy walking up the aisle and exclaimed to my shocked self: 'I'm making a commitment to live my entire life with this woman!'" Reality hit seconds before the ceremony. But Chuck and Judy have been married for 41 years and are now, at last, taking a big breath: Their youngest has just finished college.

"I married my best friend," says another happily married man I know, Tom Cunningham. "We've been married 37 years, and we're still best friends."

Each couple I talked with stressed commitment as a key to a healthy and happy marriage. Both partners also married with the certainty that they would live together for life. Consequently, they developed creative solutions for conflict resolution – and each couple did so in its own individual way. "No two persons starting married life are compatible," says John Kloeck. "Lois and I learned to be tolerant, accepting the bad as well as the good. For instance, I always worked late because we needed the money. Our first baby turned out to be twins, and we had six kids in short order. I took *every* odd job I could find.

"I did worry about money, both of us did. We married in 1937, the Depression years. There was lots of unemployment, and so we parceled out the money. I'd hand my paycheck to Lois, and she'd put it in different envelopes marked for specific purposes like shoes, groceries, or school expenses. I carried no money with me except for a couple of dollars at a time. I never took the car either. I left it for Lois, who had to handle all those kids all day long."

Money posed problems for the Barneses too. Judy quit college to work as a file clerk so Chuck could graduate from college and get better work. After three years in the Marine Corps, Chuck found employment with Scott Paper. The company moved the young couple 14 times in the first 18 years. They have been married for 41.

Judy worked the first seven years. They tried to get pregnant at first, but in time gave up and adopted a boy and, three years later, a girl. After that Judy and Chuck had three babies of their own.

Hard? Yes. Judy never finished college and often regretted it. "But," she says, "there were no easy solutions. Our marriage was important enough to persevere." Conflicts? "You bet!"

"When we married," says Tom, "I was studying for a master's in psychology which was completed the following year. Our first child was on the way. Then I taught at Seattle University, and discovered the pleasures of the classroom. I'd actually started studying to become a clinical psychologist, but then my department head suggested that I get a Ph.D.

"Even with a partial scholarship," Tom remembers, "it was scary. We had four children, the youngest only two weeks old. But we relocated and rented a house. For the first year, I taught part-time and worked part-time. After that, I taught full time, went to school full time – but always dashed home for dinner with Kathleen and the kids, helped give them baths, say prayers, and get them to bed.

"Then I'd race back to work. I completed the Ph.D. with a debt of $150 – which was borrowed from my parents. Without Kathleen's support, it would have been impossible."

In fact, each of the couples was – in today's vernacular – financially challenged. And in each case, the husband worked or studied full time, while the wife managed the money and stayed home with the children. Probably that wouldn't pan out today. Indeed, it didn't always work that way in the old days, either. My own mother stayed home until my sister entered school, and then began working full time again as a teacher. And that was all the way back in 1924.

But regardless of the situation, or even the times, one fact remains: The early years of marriage are punctuated with hardships and misunderstandings. "It was difficult to make ends meet," says Judy Barnes. "Even later on, we had to say No to the kids a lot. But they understood why. We never took an expensive vacation."

And yet another thing becomes apparent in talking to these couples: None of them wasted time brooding and nursing old wounds. Rather, each spouse pondered the unique wonder of the other's existence – insofar as they had time to consider anything. "Did you regret not finishing college?" I asked Judy. "Yes," she said. "Especially in my younger years." When I put the question to Chuck, he remembered that Judy has occasionally stormed at him for not having had time to complete her undergraduate degree.

Though all the partners acknowledged some disappointments, all made concessions to make one another's big dreams come true. When Kathleen Cunningham returned to school to get her degree and become a registered nurse, for instance, Tom re-arranged his schedule to be home with the kids in the morning and get them off to school. "Tom," says Kathleen, "always did anything I asked."

Tolerance is also essential in marriage. "Lois," John Kloeck says, "is very tolerant."

And the challenges go deeper than that. "Both of us came from dysfunctional homes," Chuck Barnes explains. "Judy's father walked out on her mother, and left her with nine children. My own father died when I was six months old, and they weren't married anyway." Consequently, these couples found over the years that there was a place in their lives for prayer. "Never has a day gone by," Chuck says, "that I haven't prayed for us, and especially prayed for Judy's happiness. Of course we've had disagreements, but even then I prayed for *us*."

"Kathleen," Tom reiterates, "is still my best friend."

John and Lois agreed on a particular condition for their friendship: "Never go to bed angry."

"We learned how to live together," they say. And, despite John's fixed feelings that he didn't want his wife working, Lois did take part-time jobs to help with the tight finances.

Another important component of a good marriage, according to the Cunninghams, is sharing. "We shared our faith life," Kathleen says. "We shared values. We knew what to overlook in each other and the kids, and what to stand up for. We respect each other and make room for differences."

"A mixed marriage does pose problems," John Kloeck acknowledges. But it turned out not to be much of a problem in the long run. "Lois was at least as good a Catholic as I when we married," John says, even though she was officially of a different faith. "She taught catechism to our children, and drove them to the 6:30 a.m. Mass to be altar servers. One day a Sister at the kids' school said, 'You know the catechism. Why not become a Catholic?' And Lois did. We communicated about faith issues, developed mutual understanding and mutual caring love."

Both the Kloecks and Barneses put their children through Catholic schools and college. The Cunninghams sent their children primarily to public schools because parochial schools were not well integrated at that time, and they wanted their children to experience an interracial environment.

In retrospect, though, John and Lois Kloeck wonder how they ever managed raising their brood. They agree it was due, in no small part, to the fact that they were a team.

And each couple has some special memory from all their years of marriage. For John and Lois, it's pigs. John always worked other angles besides his regular job. And, in fact, as a microbiologist in a tuberculosis research lab in Chicago, he once found himself with an order for 200 unborn piglets.

First, John found some big tanks and stored them in their basement. Then, he went to the stockyards and collected the necessary pig fetuses after the sows were butchered. These he dropped into the formaldahyde-filled tanks he'd put in the basement. But first, he and Lois had to inject dyes into the piglets' veins and arteries. And then, when they finally had 200, the company that had placed the order no longer wanted them!

Finally the young couple did manage to sell their carefully prepared piglets to an outfit that resold the troublesome surplus to universities for biology classes. John and Lois, meanwhile, were much relieved: Lois was pregnant at the time, and the 200 piglets paid for all the medical and birth care bills.

The couples have endured other challenges, too. Recently Tom developed a unique hobby, one that was not all that thrilling to Kathleen. He built a house on Washington's Whidby Island to serve as a hideaway. But then Tom discovered he didn't enjoy the hideaway. What he *really* enjoyed was *building* the hideaway!

So he bought two more lots. Then he built another house, and yet another. Kathleen helped with the first, and so did all of their friends. But everybody – particularly Kathleen – was a little less supportive of Tom's second and third building sprees. Tom, on the other hand, realized he'd discovered an outlet with no relation to psychology: building! Kathleen, meanwhile, enjoys her nursing and has her own special interests as well.

These days, Judy Barnes is extremely busy also. As executive director for Shepherd's Counseling Services – my non-profit therapy clinic – she has helped keep us financially afloat through difficult times. Chuck, retired after 35 years with his company, now owns his own executive search firm.

Through it all, the couples say, religious faith grounded, nourished, and guided them through the challenges of four, five, or six decades of marriage.

And even the religion arena called for concessions. "I liked the five o'clock Mass on Saturday," says Chuck, "but Judy always went to the nine on Sunday. On Sunday mornings I could sleep a bit late, and then get in a good run. We discussed the subject many times. Yes, it would be nice to attend Mass together, but I wanted that extra rest and run.

"However, as I pondered it all, I realized the value of attending Mass together, as a family. And so I changed to the nine on Sunday – and I still get in the six-mile run."

Chuck's brief story is a paradigm of problem-solving. It has a familiar ring, too. The same stories of sharing and more are told by John and Lois Kloeck and Kathleen and Tom Cunningham. These are the things all three couples have in common – along with good marriages.

SUMMARY

Marriage isn't easy, and even couples who have enjoyed long, happy unions readily admit to having weathered tough times. Yet, there are several traits all healthy partnerships have in common. They include sharing things, respecting one another, and being friends.

Highlights

- An ability to resolve conflicts without holding grudges is a big key to strong marriages.
- Shared values, if not shared faiths, are important for upholding lifelong commitments.
- Handling financial matters equitably leads to equal partnerships.
- Being able to recall memories together helps keep the spark of attraction glowing between two people.

Discussion

1. What characteristics of the marriages described in this chapter impress you most? Why?

2. Are there any elements of conflict mentioned here that you have struggled with in your ownrelationships? Which ones? Which good partnership habit do you think poses the biggest challenge for you? Why? How do you plan to overcome it?

3. How can every marriage be improved? What factor, in your opinion, is most crucial to buildinga happy marriage? How can this trait best be nurtured between two people who love each other?

FIFTEEN

Working Your Way Back from Tough Times

Nora Salah felt hopeless.

And tired. So very tired.

Nora had fled from her native Somalia to a refugee camp in Nairobi, Kenya. In the camp, there was never enough food for Nora or her husband or, for that matter, any of the other displaced persons who shared their ramshackle accommodations. Finally, World Relief Services gave Nora and her husband plane tickets to the United States. In exchange, they had to agree to pay back the ticket cost. But once in America, Nora's husband would not let Nora work to help honor their commitment. And he began to abuse her.

Worse, Nora was doubly vulnerable: Not only was she an unskilled woman in a foreign land, she was hearing impaired. Amid all the military strife in Somalia, Nora Salah and her family had found themselves caught in the crossfire. One day a bomb exploded and Nora had the misfortune of being too close to its incendiary noise. Now, she was permanently hard of hearing. Worse still, she'd lost the one person she could count on when her mother was murdered by rival factions.

All alone in America, Nora found she had absolutely no place to go or no one to turn to. Her English was poor. She had no money. Never having been allowed to work, she didn't even know how to hold a job or go about getting one.

And so Nora found herself in a battered women's shelter in St. Paul, Minnesota. A faithful Muslim, Nora had never stopped praying – particularly in her moments of need. Indeed, probably all Nora had going for her right now was God. God, of course, did not let her down. For her part, Nora Salah never expected that God might.

Meanwhile, on the other side of St. Paul, a telephone was ringing. When Sister Elizabeth answered, she found a social worker on the line. The worker was calling from the battered women's shelter.

"We have," the woman told Sister Elizabeth, "a woman who needs your RoseCenter program." Then the advocate described Nora's desperate situation.

Sister Elizabeth accepted Nora into her program then and there. After all, RoseCenter, a residential treatment center for women with no resources, was created with people like Nora in mind.

Located in a small apartment building in St. Paul, RoseCenter is operated by the Good Shepherd Sisters. It accommodates a maximum of eight or nine single women, ages 18 to 24, at a time.

Its goal? To prepare them for employment and financial independence. Obtaining education, career development assistance, financial management skills, personal development, and permanent housing are priorities at RoseCenter.

Some women may come to RoseCenter from foster-care at age 18 with no employable skills. Others are immigrants, refugees, or homeless women who simply can't find jobs.

All, however, have one thing in common in spite of their diverse backgrounds: Nobody is admitted to RoseCenter unless she is committed to self-improvement. Naturally, no drugs or alcohol are allowed.

For her part, Nora was grateful for the opportunity RoseCenter offered. But she was daunted by it, too. "I was scared," she says today. "I had come from a war-torn country. I didn't know I had tuberculosis, but that's why I was always tired. It's gone now because I was treated for it for two years. And RoseCenter helped me find a doctor to treat my hearing loss also. I've had two surgeries."

But Nora's problems weren't limited to physical disabilities. She had a lot of cultural catching up to do as well. "I didn't know how to ride the city bus," she explains, "or count money. Sister Elizabeth rode buses with me, taught me to read bus schedules, explained U.S. money.

"I learned how to read and write at RoseCenter, too," Nora says. "Throughout this time, I couldn't pay for anything. I certainly had no money of my own. But even if I had, I was still too scared to take care of myself.

"But I never stopped praying. I always prayed. Though I'm a Muslim, and Sister Elizabeth is a Christian, it never made any difference. We've made progress together.

"I didn't do well for a long time," Nora says now, "but nobody beat me down like my husband had. Nevertheless, for a long time I felt so confused. I figured they wanted *something* out of me. But nobody did. I went to English classes, and Sister found me a tutor. Little by little I got my life back. I made friends. It was too good to be true. But now I understand: God arranged all this for me.

"Today, I'm working. Me! I have a job in America! I help elderly people in their homes. And I get paid for it."

"Women often come into our program needing some initial help from the state," Sister Elizabeth says, "but they go on to become financially independent."

Nora Salah isn't RoseCenter's only success story. Far from it.

Ngan was born an Amerasian in Vietnam. Consequently, she was scorned, even by her own mother. Then when Ngan was five, her mother brought her to a harbor. "Wait for me," the woman said. She never came back.

A Vietnamese soldier picked up the child when nobody else did. He made her work, and beat her a lot. Ngan grew up scrounging for scraps of food, keeping out of the way. She had no birth certificate so she could not go to school. When possible, she dug up the backpacks that American soldiers had left behind, buried in out-of-the-way places. Usually, there were crackers with peanut butter in the backpacks, and Ngan was hungry.

Eventually, Ngan was sold into slavery.

For the next two years, things only got worse. "I suffered terribly," remembers Ngan. "Children teased and taunted me, and I got beatings." When the United States finally opened up immigration for mixed-race Vietnamese children from the war, the family who'd bought Ngan filled out the necessary papers. They weren't looking out for Ngan, though. In fact, they were hoping they, too, could emigrate.

Ultimately, Ngan received some small measure of justice when she was allowed to come to the U.S., but the family who owned and mistreated her was not.

With this move, life did become better for Ngan. First, she was placed with a loving and supportive foster family in the Midwest. And later, after a Vietnamese Good Shepherd Sister became her case-manager, Ngan was admitted to RoseCenter's independent living skills program.

At RoseCenter, Ngan received her own room, clean clothes, and good food. She went to school where she studied English as a second language. Through medical assistance she got health care, and received welfare for two months.

But Ngan never wanted to be on welfare. After the initial subsidy, she didn't require it, either. As soon as she obtained work in a sewing factory, Ngan began saving money – penny by penny. Before long, she had $2,000 saved.

Today Ngan has a happy marriage and a child. Family is very important in the Vietnamese culture, so she asked several Good Shepherd Sisters to be the baby's grandmothers; they happily agreed.

At least eight in ten RoseCenter residents achieve financial independence. Some women cannot continue at RoseCenter because of alcohol/drug addiction, or serious emotional problems. When that happens, referrals are made to the appropriate treatment facilities.

Says Sister Elizabeth, "The old assumption that everybody can pull him- or herself up by the bootstraps does not apply to women who come to RoseCenter.

"The women we see," she explains, "have been so damaged by abuse, neglect, chemical addiction, and inadequate parenting that they need individual support. They need that encouragement which values each individual as precious in God's sight, and appreciates her ability to change her life. Current belief in sanctions and regulations can be helpful, but constitute only a small part of the overall solution."

To be sure, just as Nora and Ngan are by no means RoseCenter's only success stories, RoseCenter itself is not a one-of-a-kind helping hand to the many down-and-out people who want to help themselves.

Consider Tilly. A Denver couple adopted Tilly from a Vietnamese orphanage. When she was four, her mother had a car accident that totally disabled the woman. Her father cared for Tilly as best he could, and then remarried. The child and her stepmother competed for attention, but Tilly lost. Her father, who had a drinking problem and a brain injury, was a stern disciplinarian.

At age 16, Tilly ran away with her boyfriend. They had a child.

Because her boyfriend drank too, Tilly and her baby moved on. After they found low-cost housing in a facility run by the Mercy Sisters, Tilly started college on a scholarship. With welfare and a child-care package, she was holding an associate degree within two years.

Before long, Tilly was a case manager for women with problems – women not unlike Tilly in days gone by. But the unresolved trauma of Tilly's childhood now began to chip away at her. Tilly struggled to cope, but it was an uphill battle: She just had too many problems herself.

Fortunately, Tilly knew something about social services by now; after all, she was successfully working in the field. And so she found Maria Droste, a counseling service in Denver named after Blessed Maria Droste, a Good Shepherd Sister. Tilly, like everybody else who visits Maria Droste, began receiving psychotherapy on an ability-to-pay basis.

"I wanted counseling," says Tilly, who was totally aware of the troubles she faced but just needed some guidance in doing so. "I wanted counseling not just for myself, but for my son and my family. I hated myself, and believed the world hated me, too. I was frightened, angry, and bitter. "I couldn't love my baby," she explains matter-of-factly, "because I had no love to give. And my child was developing problems as a result. I simply didn't know how to be a mom. I had never learned to love."

At Maria Droste, Sister Marge Cashman changed all that. "She gave me unconditional love and respect," says Tilly. "It was my first experience of genuine love.

"Gradually," Tilly explains, "through therapy, I developed some sense of self, a self-concept, and acquired inner-strength. Then, with Sister Marge's help, I learned about God, and God's love for me. I tried to experience that love, even to feel it. As I became conscious of God's love for me, I became able to give love to my child.

"In May of '93, I got off welfare. It was scary," Tilly admits. "Now, though, I work as an airline reservationist, and I feel satisfied because I'm doing it on my own. Getting off welfare is like winning a war. You look at each obstacle, and wonder how to cope with it."

But Tilly has learned to cope. And how! It took years of hard work, however, and a lot of psychotherapy. Tilly never wanted help from the system. Reluctantly, she did accept some welfare, and then made it on her own.

Today, she attends college part-time in addition to her job. And she continues to revel in the unconditional love she receives from social worker Sister Marge Cashman at Maria Droste. "Nobody accepted me before," Tilly says, "so I figured God didn't either. Marge gave me unconditional love, and so I can love others now."

Sally found Maria Droste, too – and it wasn't by chance. Then again, unlike Tilly's Droste experience, Sally's arrival there wasn't exactly voluntary, either. The Denver Courts ordered Sally to Maria Droste for counseling. Indeed, a social service worker accompanied Sally to Droste on her first visit. It was the social worker's job as well to make sure Sally attended the AA meetings that also were mandated by the Court. In addition, the social worker was responsible for custody of Sally's infant son, and repeatedly checked on her progress.

At first, Sally resented her loss of freedom. "I hated it," she says.

But Sally was homeless and alcoholic, and she had a baby.

That was in early 1991. Back then, Sally was on welfare with no other income, and lived in subsidized housing. "I felt pressured," she recalls. "The Court followed me every day, at least that's how it seemed. In retrospect, I was given an opportunity for tremendous growth. I had no idea how sick I was, or how much I needed healing.

"Maria Droste charges on a sliding scale, so at first I paid only $3 a session.

"The therapists figured out my issues, and brought them up in sessions," she continues. "I didn't want to know about them or face them.

"AA helped too," Sally notes, "but in a different way. AA continues to be the basis for my sobriety and spiritual growth. AA, however, does not deal with my most severe problems: childhood incest and extremely low self-esteem. Nevertheless, AA is my life. I begin each day now with meditation and am nourished by spirituality. And my therapy never clashed with AA. I needed that therapy to heal from a painful past.

"It changed my self-image. We also worked on parenting issues. Obviously, I tried to parent as my mom and stepmom had – and their methods were disastrous. So I needed to learn how to be a mom, and acquiring those skills became part of therapy, a part of my education in breaking the cycle of abuse."

Now, Sally sits on the Board of Directors of the housing development where she once lived on welfare.

"My sense of self-sufficiency comes from God," Sally says. But the Lord helps those who help themselves, and Sally has done that, too. "After my Court-mandated therapy concluded," she explains, "I chose to continue to become self-sufficient, emotionally wise, and trust myself. I've received several awards, too, which certainly helped boost my self-esteem and confidence."

Indeed, Sally was voted Woman to Watch in 1994 by the League of Women Voters because she'd come from homelessness to living a good life with her child. Today, she's a registered nurse. "I always give back," Sally says, "and that's a key to my success.

"When I reflect on the hours of therapy that gave me a new life," she says, looking back, "I value the safe place created for me, where I could cry, discuss problems impossible to talk about elsewhere, learn how to trust, and parent my child.

"Maria Droste was integral to the change in my life," Sally explains, "because of the sliding-scale fees and the flexibility they offered in suiting my unique needs.

"The journey off welfare into education, a professional life, and self-esteem and self-trust was long but most rewarding."

"Empowering women to move from welfare to work," says Good Shepherd Sister Marge Cashman, "is not the quick and simple solution most Americans want it to be. After 16 or 26 years of hearing: 'You're no good. You'll never amount to anything,' you cannot unlearn the messages in six sessions or even six months.

"Women need mentors, community resources, and therapists who commit to their well-being and growth *until* they can stand on their own in a network of peer supports," Cashman says. "*Then* they can internalize new messages: 'I am gifted. I am important. I am loveable.' Then, and *only* then can they risk trying new behaviors, new training, and job experiences."

SUMMARY

Living the good life is more than a matter of dollars and cents. A lot more. After years of hearing: "You can't," we don't unlearn the negative messages overnight. Indeed, it can take years of hearing "You can" before some people can even work up the courage to *try* to help themselves. Unfortunately, hard work isn't the only answer. We need psychotherapy to figure out the *why* of our lives, why things were they way they were in our childhoods, why we learned the things we did (or didn't!), why our lives became such a mess. We may need role models to replace self-defeating behaviors with empowering ones. We may need education to round out the missing pieces in our past schooling, we may need therapy to learn to love ourselves when we never were taught how loveable we are in the first place.

Highlights

- Social action programs are crucial if the marginalized members of our society are to "pull themselves up by their bootstraps."
- Childcare, professional instruction, and professional psychotherapy cost money. Those who are most disadvantaged tend to need these services the most.
- We parent our children the way we ourselves were parented. This can leave us with good feelings and healthy self-esteem — or an unfortunate, at times extremely damaging, example.

Discussion

1. Why can't everybody just pull him- or herself up by the bootstraps?
2. Have you ever been in a tough situation when you needed help from somebody? Did you ask for help? Why or why not?
3. Can asking for help when you need it actually be a strength rather than a weakness? How?
4. Which character in this chapter do you most admire? Why?

SIXTEEN

How to Succeed

"You can be whatever you want," my father used to tell me. "You can do whatever you want to do." He was right. I could, I did, and I do.

That statement is true for me, for you, and for the whole world. Time after time I've watched clients pick themselves up and then forge lives of incredible success. I've also had the great fortune to know a number of humble folks who, in their own quiet ways, did big things as well.

And one of the most unusual stories of persons accomplishing great deeds against incredible odds is something I've witnessed with my own eyes in Portland, Oregon.

It all began on a desolate inner-city street: Portland's Burnside Avenue, a place progress had forsaken. Once, downtown Portland was a thriving community with hotels, shops, and cheerful meeting places. But over time, as in most big cities, Old Town wilted. Without resources and economic support, Old Town turned into a home for those whose home is no place. Entire sections of Burnside gave way to bustling drug bazaars. The streets became a receptacle for the abused and the addicted, the lonely and the desperate.

But through it all, Sixth and Burnside – one little corner of an otherwise troubled neighborhood – has remained something more than a drug market. Since 1919, this location has been home to the Downtown Catholic Chapel.

No spire, dome, or vaulted ceilings here, however. The Downtown Catholic Chapel is marked only by a statue of Jesus, rising 15 feet above street level, arms outstretched in blessing. A pedestrian could pass the spot a dozen times without a clue that a church lies inside, or without glancing up at the statue.

Only a few months ago I myself walked into Downtown Chapel, thinking it was some kind of warehouse. There I met Donald, a diabetic, who has problems with his legs. He was deeply troubled by the recent death of his friend, Jack. "I was a heavy alcoholic for 25 years," Donald explained, "and Jack got me off. Now he's dead of alcoholism."

Then, slowly, Donald smiled. There is one bright spot in his life. "I was out of the Church for years," he said, "and now I attend Mass every Sunday. I love it."

Sister Elsie Fields knows Donald well – and a lot of others like him.

But this Sister of the Good Shepherd Order remembers Bob, in particular. Bob lived outdoors – in an Oregon field. When he heard that Portland's Downtown Chapel was giving away food, Bob hitchhiked 20 miles from Gresham with a backpack and a sleeping bag.

When Bob arrived at the Downtown Chapel, a volunteer made him a sandwich and filled a bag with bananas, canned juice, fruit cocktail, and pork and beans. Bob thanked her. Then he sat in the lobby and ate every bit of food in the bag. He was one hungry man.

The Good Shepherd Sisters remember Dora, too. Dora came to the Macdonald Center, operated by Portland's Downtown Chapel ministry, looking for a warm jacket. She looked about 40, but was actually 25. Sister Cathie Boerboom spent hours listening to Dora's long story and offered suggestions for jobs. But Sister Cathie knew that life was not likely to improve for Dora; Dora was mentally ill and needed a supportive environment. The streets of Portland were not likely to provide this.

In a purse tied about her waist, the woman kept her ID and a little money. But when Dora left Macdonald Center for a nearby coffee shop, she discovered her purse was gone.

Upon leaving Sister Cathie, Dora had simply laid her purse on the top layer of her backpack instead of placing it in her waist pouch. And somebody had wasted no time in lifting it. People with mental-health problems are expected to make it on their own, Sister Cathie explains, and they do try. But often, they just can't.

All this outreach to the poor on Burnside began one day in 1990 when Father Richard Berg, pastor of Portland's Downtown Chapel, stood in his office looking out the window, surveying the environs beyond. Look as he might, the priest could not locate a single family dwelling. Yet he knew that some 12,000 to 13,000 persons lived within his parish boundaries. All were quartered in single rooms in some 20 hotels set up for low-cost housing, in drug and alcohol treatment centers, in the two jails, in doorways, under bridges, and in abandoned buildings.

That Burnside was a neighborhood in trouble was common knowledge. Several years earlier, in fact, Burnside's concerned citizens had joined in an effort to reclaim their streets. Consequently, a neighborhood association had evolved: local businesses, leaders from Chinatown, Father Richard and others from the Downtown Chapel, as well as Portland's Central City Concern, the police, and other public officials galvanized to deal with the problems of gangs, drugs, violence, and disruption.

Now, as the current coordinator of the Neighborhood Association, Father Richard realized his parishioners needed even more. And so, in 1990, in the Downtown Chapel basement, he began developing the small beginnings of an outreach ministry. Today that ministry is called the Macdonald Center. But six years ago, the effort was only a dream: with a couple of volunteers, the Holy Cross priest simply hit the mean streets to offer friendship and such help as he could give.

Then in 1992, Father Richard learned that Oregon's Good Shepherd Sisters were researching ways in which their Order might better serve the poor women and children of Portland. So Father Richard sat down for a talk with the Good Shepherd Sisters, with the priest outlining Burnside's most pressing needs, needs he'd witnessed firsthand.

He told the Sisters, for example, about a woman he met in the chapel one day.

"Might I drop in and sit quietly?" she asked.

"Of course," he said.

"I'm a prostitute," the woman said quickly.

"You're welcome in Downtown Chapel," responded Father Richard.

The priest certainly understood the dangers for women on the streets. The Macdonald Center, he explained to the Sisters, needed to focus especially on the women and children of Burnside. It was only logical to join forces. And so by the end of 1992, two Good Shepherd Sisters, Elsie and Cathie, were working the streets of Burnside, building the Macdonald Center ministry along with Father Richard.

But *money!*

Father Richard needed money to develop and continue the Macdonald Center.

Dean of the psychology department at the University of Portland when he started Macdonald Center, Berg first put the question of funding to his students.

"What's the best way to do it?" he asked.

"Collect pennies for the poor," one suggested.

Pennies! Fund the efforts to reclaim Burnside and offer assistance to the hundreds of poor persons on that street – with pennies!

Father Berg and the Sisters saw a need. But they lacked resources. So they set out to do what they wanted to do: one penny at a time.

In a very short time, in fact, Father Richard had Catholic schools and parishes all over Portland turning his Pennies for the Poor program into parish Advent campaigns. The first year alone, $7,000 in pennies were collected. The number doubled in 1993. And doubled again in 1994 . . . to the tune of $55,000. All in pennies.

Indeed, the '94 campaign was boosted in part by an innovation above and beyond the old penny drive. Children at Holy Redeemer Grade School – the Good Shepherd Sisters' own parish – gave themselves a new challenge: They would, they decided, raise *one ton* of pennies. And they did.

It's a far cry from the Macdonald Center's humble beginnings. And the Good Shepherd Sisters have by no means forgotten what those days were like. In their first winter at Macdonald Center, the Sisters trekked across the parish – on foot – with their Meals on Heels program. They pushed carts through snow and ice, bringing food to the residents of Burnside's low-cost hotels.

Along the way, the Sisters would meet with persons in treatment centers and jails. On sidewalks, they'd chat with pedestrians.

As they conversed with people, Sister Elsie and Sister Cathie tried to discern if the individuals needed food, a physician, a mental-health counselor, clothing, or some other kind of assistance. They did their best to hook people up with available agencies and resources.

Today, the Macdonald Center employs seven workers. Along with some 80 volunteers, the staff maintains a warm haven, offering coffee and conversation for the homeless and others in need. And Macdonald Center workers still walk the streets, two by two.

Primarily, they listen. The 12,000 or so men and women who eke out a living on Burnside's streets and small, dark hotel rooms, who reside in its halls or shabby drug-treatment centers, are lonesome more than anything. Their thirst for human companionship is more compelling than even the ache for alcohol. Certainly, companionship is more difficult to obtain.

Slowly and gradually, the atmosphere on Burnside is changing. Sidewalks are friendlier. Streetwalkers smile: They have met these Sisters and volunteers before. Drug action is no longer visible; sellers and buyers have disappeared from the sidewalks.

The Neighborhood Association and Downtown chapel have taken back their streets. The Macdonald Center's staff and volunteers – mostly interns from various departments at the University of Portland – have in all given more than 10,000 hours of service to Burnside's residents last year alone. Most of the time, their greatest ministry consists of one thing and one thing only: They listen.

And they will continue to do that and more. Sister Cathie, for instance, recalls the day she and Sister Elsie, walking the streets, noticed a station wagon with several children in it, the oldest not more than ten. Two or three scruffy-looking men were eyeing the car, circling it. It was winter, and it was cold, but the Sisters knew they had to stay close to that car. And they did – for 30 minutes.

Then the children's father came hurrying from a nearby building and asked the Sisters for directions so he could pay his electric bill. He had searched through the adjacent buildings, hoping to find the proper office there. He *had* to pay that day, he explained, or his electricity would be turned off. The Sisters gave him directions. Then they advised him never to leave his children alone in a car again. They told him why. A recent immigrant, the man had not suspected the danger.

Sometimes women the Sisters meet on Burnside Avenue ask: "Why should I go on living? I have nobody left."

"Because," the Sisters always say, "*we* love you."

And so it happens that every Friday night the two Sisters – each with a Macdonald Center volunteer – walk Portland's downtown streets in search of people who need help. The Sisters provide blankets for those who are cold. They get medical help for those who are sick. They feed the hungry.

Not long ago a homeless man stood outside the Downtown Chapel and stared at the statue of Jesus for some 15 minutes.

"You know," the man said, "that Jesus looks handsome and strong. And with his arms stretched out the way they are, it looks like He's saying, 'Come on in. I'll take care of you.'

"I can just tell," the man said, "that this Jesus would never put anyone down."

And neither would anybody at Portland's Macdonald Center, or at the Downtown Chapel, or at the Burnside Neighborhood Association. *Penny by penny*, and hug by hug, these groups – thanks to the dedicated people who run them – have taken back the city's mean streets.

Father Berg had a dream. The Good Shepherd Sisters had a dream. And together they turned their dream into a reality. One penny at a time.

How true were my father's words spoken so many years ago: "You can be whatever you want to be. You can do whatever you really want to do."

SUMMARY

Success begins with us. By examining the ways in which others have accomplished big things with few resources, we can gain insight on how we might do big things with our own lives. Even if it means starting out on a small scale, beginning our life's projects by simply defining them and then embarking on the journey, we *can* obtain our goals. But we must set out to achieve them one step at a time.

Highlights

- Most people who succeed believe in themselves.
- Doing things one step at a time, doing what we can in the here and now, is the formula for reaching big goals in incremental stages. Then, all the small steps will build, one upon the other, creating a ladder we might climb to obtain success in the big picture of life.

- It's better to focus not so much on how big is the job that must be done, but on what we can do now to make something positive happen, what we can do now to take one step forward toward our dream.

Discussion

1. Why did Father Richard Berg and the Good Shepherd Sisters succeed?

2. What role does self-esteem play in success?

3. Is there something you want to accomplish? Write it down. Can you think of a realistic plan to start making things happen for yourself – one step at a time?

4. Have you given yourself permission to succeed? Can you do that . . . right now?

SEVENTEEN

To Pray Best:
Keep It Simple

Throughout life, I have worked with teenagers and clients who don't belong to any church. Too often, the only time some of these teens have heard God's name was in cursing and swearing. And yet, deep within every client I have ever known – *particularly* the unchurched – lies a rich, internal spirituality impatient for birth. Sometimes I listen to men and women who have never prayed, never stepped inside a church, never read a word of the Bible – and yet, unknowingly, they have been searching for God. Sooner or later that timid quest is put into words.

"I talked to God," the frightened person seated before me says one day.

"It's all right," I always reassure the client. "It's OK. The rest of the journey is up to God." Marvelously, God lets me help.

Prayer is simply a conversation, a looking at God. And when we talk about prayer, I find myself looking to role models of my own. (Even we psychologists have got to learn from somebody!)

And one person I particularly respect and admire, from whom I have learned a great deal about prayer, is Sister Edna.

Sister Edna lives prayer, an essentially simple prayer without words. Because so many of my clients ask, "How do I pray?" I'll share Sister Edna's words on prayer.

As a young woman growing up in her native Egypt, Edna Ashamalla joined the Roman Catholic Church from her Coptic Orthodox faith. Her parents, wealthy professionals in Cairo, as well as her four brothers and two sisters, were dismayed.

She certainly would not, she knew, get permission for what she really wanted: to become a Roman Catholic Religious, a Good

Shepherd Sister. Edna was familiar with the way of life of these women because they had taught her in school.

But since becoming one of them was impossible for now, she enrolled in engineering school. Edna was biding her time until age 21, when she would be legally free to make her own decisions.

When that day came, however, her family still did not relent. At that point, Edna made up her mind to travel to France anyway; there, she entered the Good Shepherd novitiate. Her father, broken-hearted, died two years later; her dismayed mother would not speak to Edna for eight years. And Edna, who dearly loved her family, suffered keenly from the rupture.

Fortunately, Edna and her father did reconcile before he died. Her mother, brothers, and sisters took a while longer to accept Edna's vocation. Indeed, in time they even began helping her in her work.

Still, while her vocation was to the Good Shepherd – a very active group of Religious – Edna longed for a contemplative life, for a quiet corner of the world alone with God.

"But everyone I asked for advice," she explains, "told me, 'You can't be a contemplative. You love sports, dancing, education. No. You belong in the active life.'

"Yet deep within," Sister Edna says, "I longed for contemplation, time with Jesus alone."

In time, Sister Edna returned to Egypt, first as principal of the biggest Good Shepherd school in Cairo where she was given charge of more than 1,500 students. Then she was appointed director of all Good Shepherd schools in Egypt: two more in Cairo with about 500 students each, three more in Port Said, and one in Suez. Next, she was named regional superior of all Good Shepherd Sisters and their works in both Egypt and Sudan.

"But," she remembers, "I was brought up on the Desert Fathers, in the contemplative tradition. So whenever I had time to think, particularly when I made retreats, I longed for silence, stillness, a quiet space alone with God."

The contemplative branch of the Good Shepherd Sisters, though, has no convent in the Middle East. In 1993, therefore, Sister Edna traveled to St. Louis, Missouri, and joined the Good Shepherd Contemplatives there.

"Are you happy?" I asked her recently.

"Blissful," she replied.

How does she pray now that her whole life is prayer?

"Prayer," she explains, "is the very essence of our vocation. I join our little community of Sisters in daily prayer in our chapel for Eucharist, the center of our lives; we also pray the Liturgy of the Hours five times a day, along with the Angelus; we pray before and after meals; we practice holy or prayer hours and contemplation of the Blessed Sacrament on Sundays and the eve of solemn Feasts. We have private prayers, too: an hour of daily meditation, spiritual reading, short visits to the Holy Sacrament, the rosary. We receive the sacrament of reconciliation frequently. We devote time to recollection and prayer at least one day a month, plus an annual retreat of seven or more days."

How does Sister Edna pray most often when she is alone? "For private prayer," she says, "I like to meditate with icons, especially the icon of the Holy Trinity. We don't really need to think, read, or hunt for words with God. We need only look and listen: And I look with eyes closed because a familiar icon is a friend."

Why does Sister Edna pray?

"Jesus is my friend, the dearest friend I own," she tells me. "I need to share with him, moment by moment. To dial his number is, for me, to recall an Icon. Rublev's Holy Trinity is named the *Welcome*, the *Reception*, because it's an invitation to live in the Home of Love, the Heart of the Trinity. Once there I only point to what's happened to family and friends: perhaps divorce, bankruptcy, illness, death. I simply look at the persons who ask for our prayers, as well as the Church, our pope, our clergy, and our congregations, and then I look out to the whole world where there may be catastrophies, disasters, wars, violence. And I look especially to the poor, the weak, the persecuted and the oppressed, and those served by our active Good Shepherd Sisters.

"I let Jesus know my joys, and I thank Jesus for the graces and blessings given to all people," Sister Edna explains. "Especially I thank him for calling me to contemplative life, and to the loving Sisters in our Convent. God is present in the heart of the world, in the pain – but God is also present within our gladness and happiness.

"At Cana, Mary simply points out the fact: They have no wine. Likewise, I don't need words for prayer. I reach out to the Trinity and open to them my heart, feelings, emotions, trust, and abandonment to their love. God knows what we need. God wants us to express in silence our faith, trust, and gratitude."

What does Sister Edna hear in prayer?

"I listen and hear God's words to Isaiah: 'Come to me . . . stay with me,' and you will have consolation and peace. 'Fear not for I am with you,' and with my people. 'You are precious in my eyes . . . I love you,' as I love all who suffer. 'No one will be lost . . . I will save all those given me by the (Creator).' I listen, and peace fills my heart."

What has Edna learned in her prayer?

"We don't need much time to reach God," she reassures us. "We need develop only one or two small devotions such as the name of Jesus and the sign of the cross.

"As I cut hosts in the altar bread room, for example, I say 'Jesus' with each pull on the cutter machine, about 500 times an hour. Also, when I stamp our return address or the word 'Fragile' on boxes to mail altar breads to our customers, I say 'Jesus' with each stamping, about 150 times an hour. Although busy throughout the morning, I pray constantly. We pray by pronouncing the name of Jesus. That name becomes vibrantly alive with all our feelings: love, respect, admiration, friendship. The name of Jesus fills hearts with gladness, mouths with praise. Scientifically we could say that the name of Jesus carries an electric charge.

"I breathe the name of Jesus while doing ordinary actions like washing my face, going up and down stairs, walking, in the elevator, waiting for the Doctor. Wherever we go, we can repeat that holy name. That name is presence and power.

"Another devotion," continues Sister Edna, "is the sign of the cross. The first Christians were devoted to that sign. Tertullian said: 'At every forward step and movement, going in or out, when we put on our clothes and shoes, when we bathe, when we sit at table, when we light the lamp, or sit – in all the ordinary actions of everyday life we trace upon the forehead the sign of the cross.'

"I try with patience and perseverance to develop the habit of praying the sign of the cross. When I begin the day, or start work, help in the kitchen, cook, read a book, or write a letter, I make the sign of the cross. When changing activities, going from one place to another, zapping the TV, I make a small cross over my heart. At fixed moments in the day I invite my heart to meet God by a simple sign of the cross.

"The name of Jesus and the sign of the cross help me offer to God my life and loves. They enrich and embellish my life. They teach me how to smile at everyone I meet and put up with little pains and inconveniences. Moments spent in prayer rest our nervous systems, strengthen our spirituality, liberate us from earthly harassments, and offer us drink from springs of love.

"Anybody today – a parent at home, a teacher, a business executive, a police officer on duty – all can pray the name of Jesus and the sign of the cross. Neither devotion takes time. These simple prayers liberate the heart for genuine freedom, love, joy and happiness within the peace of the Holy Trinity."

Although I myself had met and talked with Edna at length in the past, I was unaware of her constant prayer. She's a warm, loving person. Though her words are simple and direct, the intellectual brilliance that led Edna into engineering school in Egypt, and to learn three languages, is obvious. I can't imagine a more delightful friend . . . or a better mentor for praying well.

SUMMARY

Sometimes, we have trouble finding God because we're *afraid* of God. But we don't have to be. God *made* us, and God *loves* us for *who we are*. And God wants nothing more for us than personal happiness and fulfillment – and a rich prayer life *with God*.

Highlights

- Prayer is conversation – any conversation at all – between us and God.
- Meditation, simply contemplating a holy image or word, like "Jesus," is a prayer form that we can easily fit into our less complex day-to-day activities.
- God will direct our prayer life for us. We need only desire a prayer life and ask God to help us get one started.

Discussion

1. In how many ways does Sister Edna pray? Why is she a holy person?
2. Which of Sister Edna's prayer forms might work for you? Why?
3. How might you begin working prayer into your life? Where, and how, do you plan to pray?

EIGHTEEN

Letting Go
and Letting God

Most of us can work ourselves into a frenzy about almost anything, especially if we think about it long enough. I like to ask my clients – and even myself – this question: How many problems have we actually solved by worrying about them?

I don't mean pondering, weighing, or considering. Neither do I include planning, guiding, or goal setting. The buzzword is *worry!*

What has worry ever accomplished?

Take Rob, for instance. After he began counseling with me, I asked questions about salary, expenditures, taxes, credit cards – not because I'm knowledgeable in those areas, but because Rob was clearly one very worried man. I needed to track down the more obvious sources of his worries to discover how we might deal with them.

Rob coped with worries by shutting down. Don't look, maybe they'll go away. Don't look, the consequences might terrify me. Don't look, there's not a thing I can do. Rob just worried: nameless, faceless, sleepless worries. Rob was willing to work himself to death to keep the worry monster out of sight. Sadly, he was making progress in the former, but failing miserably with the latter.

I discovered that in the year before making his appointment with me, Rob and his wife paid *$40,000 interest* on credit card debt alone. Last year, they made a combined $100,000. But they hadn't paid taxes for four years.

Now, Rob felt hopeless. And he couldn't do a thing about his troubles except worry.

Worry does that to us: It paralyzes and renders us helpless.

As Rob talked out his financial problems, though, he came to see there *were* some solutions: First of all, he set aside some time for prayer; then, he terminated all credit cards; he sold some stock to pay off the credit card debt. He and his wife also searched for their papers and records, brought them to an accountant, and got the IRS squared away. Finally, they established spending limits for themselves.

We don't always need to visit a therapist, however, to figure out what's causing us to worry ourselves into paralysis. Talking out worries with a friend often clarifies thought patterns and suggests solutions. Rather than stewing in worry, we need to consider what we might *do* to make things better. Anything.

Imagine the success we could attain if only we approached life with half the energy we expend on worry. Unfortunately science has not yet discovered a magic button to turn off worry, and I doubt that it ever will. Therefore we've got to unlearn destructive worry habits the good old-fashioned way – the hard way – one step at a time.

In unlearning worry, a good place to start is to replace the worry habit with a more productive one. Why not, for instance, replace your worried thoughts with optimistic ones? The incentive to do so is certainly a powerful one. According to University of Pennsylvania researcher Marti Seligman, quoted *Psychology Today,* the optimists among us are healthier. That's right, researchers have reason to believe that a positive outlook contributes to a stronger immune system. "Because optimism protects against illness," Seligman says, "it may help us survive." By learning to let go of worry, we can expect to live longer with more vitality.

But can we really break such a bad habit as worrying? Of course we can!

Here's How

Focus on Positive Thinking.

Whenever you catch yourself sliding into a mental tailspin of worry, *stop*! Think of three alternative outcomes to the scenario you're agonizing over. Each must be positive.

Don't Sweat the Small Stuff.

If you find yourself unable to quit worrying, ask yourself if the matter under consideration is actually worth that much worry.

Let me tell you a story: Three of us Sisters were driving back to Seattle one day after a trip to Spokane when a front tire on our car blew out. The driver managed to get the car off the freeway safely.

Immediately a car stopped behind us, and a friendly man jumped out. "I saw what happened," he said. "My mother and I don't have far to go, and we'll drive you to a garage in the next town." The Sister-driver hopped in and off they went.

Now, Spokane is in Eastern Washington. During the summer, it gets unbearably hot. Our car was parked directly in the sun, and soon we were squirming and sweating

"This is awful," my companion said. "I can't stand it. Let's pray for some relief."

Meantime, of course, we both worried lest the friendly man was not as friendly as he seemed. We realized, though, that we couldn't do anything about that now, so we quit worrying and turned it over to God.

Shortly, two cars drove up behind us. One was a garage mechanic. In the other was the mechanic's wife who came to drive us two Sisters to her own home for relief from the heat. With her was our Sister-driver.

Before long, we were sitting in an air conditioned home having tea and cookies and chatting happily while our car was repaired. Major worry for two hours could not have resolved the situation as happily as God did when we quit sweating the small stuff.

Live the Serenity Prayer.

Don't just say it. The words are beautiful: "God, grant me the serenity to accept the things I cannot change, the courage to change the things I can, and the wisdom to know the difference."

Some situations do need changing. The change may require courage, may call for our best efforts to turn matters around. Often we're the only person who can effect that change. Do we have a plan? Can we construct one?

Rose was the secretary in a local college, and she was unhappy. She had an undergraduate degree and figured she should be able to get a more challenging job. But her degree was in history, and what could she do with that? She worried that her life was deadending. I encouraged Rose to read the Want Ads, and keep reading. She might find more enjoyable and rewarding work.

Rose did discover a job offer as secretary to the head of chemical engineering at the University of Washington, and she applied. While this position was still secretarial, it offered the possibility of taking courses without having to make tuition payments. As Rose studied the course offerings, she realized that she had always wanted to learn graphic design.

Rose did get the secretarial job, and as soon as she was able, she began taking design courses. Before long, Rose had earned her graphic designer's certification and received an offer from a newspaper to become one of its staff designers. She just loves the job.

Better to expend energy on problem solving than invest it in a whirlpool of worry which can only pull us down.

Practice Serenity.

Take time, literally, to smell the roses. Look out the window. Daydream. Allow the mind to roam. Let go and let God.

Once, on a trip to Puerto Rico, I stayed with a group of American Sisters. I didn't know Spanish but my airline, Continental, offered me a free trip on mileage. The Sisters, meanwhile, assured me that getting around while there would be inexpensive and no problem: I could board any bus which passed by their school, get off, and find my way back on the same bus line.

So the morning after my arrival in Puerto Rico, I set out.

The bus took a long and winding route, certainly different from U.S. buses, but I had no reason to worry. Then the bus parked and everybody got off. I had planned on a round trip, so I tried to stay on. The driver knew no English, but he clarified that I must get off. I did so, and stood close to the bus to hop on again. But the driver went into a shop, got a lunch, and sat in the shade of the bus for what looked like a long lunch and a siesta with a group of friends. So I walked off, forward and backward, trying to find bus stops. Nothing.

I roamed and circled again. No sign of a bus, bus line, or bus stop.

I knew the Sisters' phone number, but they were away from the convent at this time of day, teaching. I could find nobody who spoke English, and had no idea where I was. I had tucked only five dollars into my wallet that morning, and knew it was insufficient for a taxi to drive me back to the Sisters.

I got tired walking, and it was very hot. Eventually I sat down on a curb. Puerto Rico is very beautiful, and I simply enjoyed the scenery – after all, there was nothing else to do.

A taxi arrived, and the driver motioned to me. I walked over, aware that I could explain nothing in Spanish. But the driver spoke English! He had been in the U.S. Army.

For four dollars he drove me to the closest bus depot. A conductor there explained that the bus I took was a rogue bus – it belonged to a man who drove it when and where he pleased. I had arrived in a totally different city than I'd intended. The conductor got me on the right bus, told me when and how to change buses, and waved me off to my destination.

My most productive action all day had been to sit and enjoy the beauty.

Take a Lesson from Scripture.

Jesus advised us not to judge lest we be judged. All my clients, however, have already judged themselves harshly by the time they walk through my door, already decided they're failures. But God made us, and God makes only the best. We – you and I – are God's most precious creation.

Do What You Can.

And then live in the present. In advocating tossing aside your worries, I'm not encouraging irresponsibility. If, like Rob, you've got a big problem on your hands, I'm not suggesting that you live in denial. If you're consumed with worry over circumstances that need addressing, you may, like Rob, need the help of an account-ant or some other professional – perhaps, even, a therapist. Too many of us, however, spend too much time worrying about those things we cannot change. And this is where we must learn to let go and let God.

Often I ask clients to take a test, the Personality Orientation Inventory, based on Maslow's hierarchy of values. I find it espe-cially useful because it measures time loss. Very often clients tell me, "I don't know where the time goes. . . ." Or they'll say: "I don't know where the morning went. . . ." Other times I hear: "I have no idea what I did last week, but I certainly didn't accomplish anything."

I once took a couple of writing classes at the University of Washington. With me were about 20 other men and women, all of whom planned to write a book. They intended to begin the actual writing in a couple of months or next year. They talked about it, made stabs at it, continued envisioning that book, but as a future actuality. Insofar as I know, only two of us ever were published: a young woman and I. We were the only ones who actually sat down, wrote the book, and looked for a publisher.

Dreaming about possibilities is fun, but God's moment is now. Today. This minute. This hour will never come again. The past is finished; the future lies in God's hands. Under God's watchful and loving eye, the present is ours.

Turn Off the Noise.

Our own inner dialogue isn't the only barrier to serenity encountered daily. Radios. Televisions. Boom boxes. The whiz-bang world we live in: noise, noise, noise. We need to find quiet time for ourselves, time when we can meditate, read, or just "be." Quietly.

I practice an hour's meditation alone with God every day. I need the silence and sense of the Divine. In fact, I can't survive without it. If I simply rush all day – and I'm very busy – my mind takes off on a whirlybird course with a jangle that unnerves me.

I worked with one young woman who had been stressed so long that every joint in her body ached. She ground her teeth at night and consequently suffered from TMJ; further, she felt hopeless about any improvement in her life.

She got up at 6 a.m., made breakfast for her two boys, got them off to school, drove to the office where she was engaged as secretary, worked until 5 p.m., drove home, got dinner on the table, washed the dishes, helped the boys with schoolwork, fell into bed, and started the same routine all over again the next day. Her husband left for work before she did, and made it home only in time for dinner.

Clearly, she needed time alone each day. We scheduled in a half-hour between 5 and 5:30, when she could listen to music, or talk to God, or just "be."

How she loved and treasured that half hour! It initiated her journey to a much less hectic lifestyle – without which she was in danger of losing her health as well as peace of mind and soul.

Forget Perfection.

"If you become perfect," I warn my clients, "you'll be a saint. And if you're a saint, you're as good as dead because God takes you saints into heaven. With perfection attained, your time on earth is over."

Many of us are perfectionists because we can't be satisfied with ourselves and our all-too-human efforts. But God does not expect the impossible of us.

The continued effort on our part to become so, however, makes us rigid, strained, and tense. When I read the lives of real saints, I discover relaxed persons ready to enjoy a good joke.

Our beloved Pope John XXIII, a genuinely holy man, enjoyed many a laugh at his own expense. I particularly enjoyed his complaint to God one day. "You knew I was going to end up on TV," the pope said, "so why did you make my nose so big, and my ears stick out?"

Discuss Your Worries with a Friend.

Sometimes naming our fears out loud takes the edge off them. That's what happens in therapy. As clients hear themselves talk about their concerns in a safe setting, they often come up with solutions to difficulties that had previously appeared insurmountable. I remember one man, probably in his 40s, who didn't know what to do with himself or where to go. His wife had divorced him, and the shock was painful.

He had headed the maintenance division at a big plant, but knew it was a job with no further promotions. He had an undergraduate degree, but never used it. As he searched for direction and talked out loud about his concerns, he came up with his own answer – one which surprised me. He decided to get a master's degree in counseling and work with teenagers. And, because he had only enough money to pay for the two years of studies with part-time work, he would trust in God to find a position as counselor.

This client got his degree, and found employment almost immediately. Today he is engaged with an agency that sends him onto the streets to work with homeless kids. He's good at it, and knows he's contributing to society.

Keep a Why-Worry? Journal.

In this notebook, friends of mine have recorded their daily progress in their quest to learn how to let go and think positive thoughts. They try to record more positive thoughts in it than negative ones. And journals need not be kept in written form alone. I've seen journals in which feelings are expressed by drawings, or photos, or illustrations cut from magazines and newspapers.

One woman I know made a journal of slides, put them together, and showed them as she told her story. Some clients have composed songs to express their feelings as they move along in life.

Journaling has helped many persons. It needs to be done consistently, however. And the journalist might reward him- or herself from time to time for the faithful entries which keep it current.

But the bottom line on journals is this: They can help us work through troubles and reassure us when we're feeling troubled. In reviewing them, we come to see that God really is in heaven and all really is OK in my world.

SUMMARY

We can waste a lot of time worrying. Indeed, the answers to life's problems often lie within us. By initiating dialogue with God, with our friends, with a therapist, some other qualified professional, or even by keeping a journal, we can better articulate the roots of our problems. When we do that, we've outlined our trouble. Now, we have only to come up with a plan. A plan that will help us keep worries at bay. And with that done, we're free to pursue serenity, to really let go and let God. When we're worried about something we cannot change, it's God's turn – not ours – to help us along. Now, our job is only to unlearn the worry habit and learn to think on God's terms. Then, God can provide.

Highlights

- Learning not to sweat the small stuff can help us attain serenity.
- We need to live the serenity prayer – not just say it.
- By unlearning our worry habit and learning to focus on positive thoughts, we not only take ourselves closer to serenity but also to God and good health.

Discussion

1. What things do you worry about? What might you do to solve these problems? Can you come up with a plan for doing so?

2. Do you worry about things you can't change? What things? What are your alternatives to worrying about these things?

3. How might you obtain some quiet time for yourself? When?

4. Can you make your own *Why-Worry Journal?* What positive thoughts will you write in it? Can you come up with at least three optimistic thoughts right now? Write them down.

NINETEEN

When We Lose a Loved One

Overwhelmed with grief, how do we move on? How do we honor the memories?

Most of us know the feeling too well. A chill sets in the heart like the old North Wind in the wintertime. When a person we love is lost to us, we can feel like we're standing alone in a freezing rain without a coat, shivering with the knowledge that the warmth inside is no longer ours to claim. Worse, in our hearts we realize that we'll never know that warmth again. Not with this special person, not in this world.

How can we go on? Do we even want to?

For a long, long time the answer may well be no. No, we don't want to go on. It's no fun being alone. It's not fair. And it's scary.

It's lonesome. The person we loved to confide in, loved to share laughter with, loved to hug, hold, and cherish is gone. The hole in our hearts is too big ever to get filled again.

When first we heard the news, when finally it began to sink in – and it didn't at first, not at first – our reaction was disbelief. It can't be. We must fix it. Strike some kind of bargain. Dicker with fate to change things around.

Inevitably, though, reality sets in. And with it comes the emptiness of a thousand sleepless nights, endless memories of regret, and – perhaps worse still – the taunting recollections spurred by the most mundane day-to-day acts. Going to the hardware store and smelling the pine boards with which you used to build things together. Walking the dog past the ice cream parlor where you both shared sodas. Smelling your favorite dish, with the esoteric spices nobody else – but the two of you – ever liked.

Is there anything good about grieving?
Yes, but we must do it well. And we must do it thoroughly.

Principles of Grieving

Grieving Takes Time.

Grief can take a lifetime to work through in all its stages: denial, anger, deep sadness. My sister died two years ago, and I miss her as keenly today as I did the day after she left me for heaven. She was a Sister of Service, a Canadian Order, and I am a Sister of the Good Shepherd, an international Order, but I'm based in the U.S.

For years I didn't see her at all: My Order was then cloistered so I couldn't travel to visit, and she spent whatever vacations she got with my parents. In the last 25 years, especially since my mother and father left for eternity, we grew very close. During the last couple of years we chatted weekly on the phone. I miss the weekly calls, I miss our vacations together, I miss the letters and cards. I miss a friend so dear that I can't think of her without tears.

Yes, I know we'll be united in heaven, but that thought does not ease the pain here and now. I have to walk through it: all of us do. I have to endure the loneliness, the sadness, the grief. And I have to allow myself time for grieving.

Get Support: Immediately and Later on.

All of us grieve differently, but none of us can shoulder grief alone. We need to rely on friends. Whenever holidays, birthdays, anniversaries come due – we need to plan ahead of time.

I particularly miss my sister at Christmas, on my birthday, on her birthday, but most keenly of all, I miss her on my annual brief vacation. For 25 years we spent our vacations – one or two weeks – together. One year we enjoyed our vacation at one of her Order's convents in Canada, and the next year we spent our time together at one of my Order's convents in the U.S. All year long we looked forward to that happy time together.

My sister died the beginning of January. I couldn't imagine what to do for my vacation that summer, 18 months ago. I absolutely could not spend vacation time in any location where we had enjoyed ourselves before. It was impossible. I dreaded vacation, yet knew I needed time off. Finally an idea hit: Go to the Good Shepherd Sisters in Panama City, Panama.

Panama is a beautiful country, but very hot. The Canal is indescribable; the ingenuity and engineering are beyond words. It must be seen.

And, even though I had never met them before, the Good Shepherd Sisters in Panama are truly sisters. Between my language problem, the Sisters' kindness, and the unfamiliar environment, I hurt less for the significant person who was absent.

Today, Good Shepherd Sisters continue to provide the quiet friendship, family, and love I need. That doesn't dull the pain, but their support makes it bearable. Each of us who loses someone we love needs to find support.

Allow Yourself Some Regrets.

Even in the best relationships we're often left wishing we could have done more. This is normal. I look back to recall many days with my sister when I should have been more loving, more understanding, more patient. Eileen spent her vacation with me only a few months before she died.

I knew she was not herself, but I was determined to get her walking, exercising, out and about. In the past, I had noted a tendency in her to give up too fast, so I encouraged her to get involved in life again – not realizing she was near the end of it. How I wish we might relive that vacation! My consolation is that she did describe those two weeks with me as "wonderful." Still, I keep telling myself that they could have been better *for her*.

To stifle the regrets is unhealthy. We will assuredly look back over the past to weep over our mistakes, our failures. The process is normal and it is all right to engage in it – and then let the regrets go.

Relish the Memories.

To live in the past is one thing. To treasure the good times is quite another. I vividly remember my first vacation with my sister, sometime in the late '60s. She brought me to an island far north of Vancouver Island on a ferry – my first ferry trip. Friends there had loaned her their vacation house.

I went swimming in the ocean (*cold!*) and lived in the ordinary fashion totally unknown to me in years of cloistered convent life. We could choose what we wanted to eat, sleep late, go to bed early. No bells for the first time in 25 years! Looking back, it was a simple vacation, but to me it was marvelous.

I remember, too, the hundreds of times we knelt at Mass together, and received Communion. The Mass had been the highlight of our lives at home, and it continued to be our most special moment throughout Eileen's life.

I think also of Eileen's regular Christmas gift to me: a ten- or twenty-dollar bill, U.S. currency. She inconvenienced herself to find that American money, and she mailed it the last Christmas, a few days before she died.

Life without her is terribly lonesome, but I do have the memories.

Get Help If You Need It.

If we've exhausted our network of friends, but still feel we can't go on, we can turn to professional help. When depression becomes paralyzing, we, being only human, need to reach out for help. I've known persons to isolate themselves in their homes after the loss of a loved one, sometimes without even adequate nutrition. I also, sadly, have known the bereaved partner left behind to consider suicide, and sometimes to have tried it.

Particularly if you're considering hurting yourself or just "putting an end to it all" in some potentially permanent way, talk about these feelings with your pastor or a trusted friend immediately. If that simply isn't possible, then pick up your phone book and look up the suicide prevention hotline number – immediately. Another option: Ask your pastor or the suicide prevention hotline professionals to refer you to a reliable mental health professional, somebody you might talk to. Remember, you are not alone. God is with you always, even when you don't feel God's presence.

Give Yourself Some Time Alone.

Well-meaning friends may almost smother us when we're mourning. It's OK to say thanks a lot, but tonight I need to be alone. Then listen to a symphony, go to the opera, work out at the gym, take in a Mass, try a retreat.

Various friends were most kind and reached out to me in several ways when my sister died. But I couldn't respond then. I still can't talk about Eileen. This chapter marks my first real attempt to write about her. My greatest need was time alone.

People differ. Some, after a great loss, want to talk it out; others, with a more private grief, need time alone. We each know ourselves best. If silent time, while engaged in varied activities, is more healing, take it.

Pray for Healing.

God knows how we suffer, and God loves each of us, individually, with a love greater than we can imagine. The best remedy when in pain, any kind of pain? God.

And please be assured, God hears every prayer. Trust me: Healing – *every type of healing* – really does happen. How do I know? I have seen it with my own eyes, felt it within my own body.

Let me tell you an amazing story:

About a year ago I developed a severe pain in my right shoulder. Week by week and month by month, the pain increased. It would not be ignored.

At first, my shoulder was encased with a dull, insidious ache. And that was bad enough. But then the ache inched down my arm, proceeding down to my fingertips. I must have pulled a muscle, I told myself, or strained a ligament. If I ignore it, it will go away.

But the pain steadily increased. The ache became a burn. Before long, I couldn't sleep on my right shoulder. Then, I couldn't sleep on my back. Unconsciously I avoided using my right arm or hand, substituting the left as much as possible. Dressing was becoming so painful that I wanted to cry, morning and evening.

The burn turned into a shooting, breath-taking sear. Finally, I quit kidding myself. I went to my doctor.

"Bursitis," he said.

I was shocked. Other people got bursitis, not me.

He was still talking: "I'll prescribe pain pills. You may need cortisone. Probably you ought to get physical therapy."

My mind was whirling, even as I stumbled out of the clinic. Bursitis! Me! I never even had arthritis!

Worse, the side effects of the pain pills turned out to be distressing. Yet I didn't want to go the cortisone route, either. And I *certainly* didn't want physical therapy: My arm and shoulder hurt too much!

"Well," I said to myself, "if I'm not able to take my doctor's advice, I'd better pray."

Shortly thereafter I received the anointing of the sick. But it certainly wasn't something I'd planned on. For centuries, this Catholic sacrament was strictly administered to persons in danger of death. In our modern era, though, even the Sacraments have been made more relevant. Now this particular blessing is acceptable for persons in need of healing, too.

But I was something of a Doubting Thomas here. After all, for most of my life, Extreme Unction (what they called it in my day) existed solely to prepare the dying for Heaven. And suddenly it was being resurrected as a Sacrament of Healing! Forget it.

Prayer? That was more my style. After these many years, I've no doubts about the power of prayer. So I stepped up my daily prayer routine, including my daily Mass habit. My bursitis was getting no better, but that didn't stop me from hoping.

And so it happened that I found myself at Mass the next First Friday of the month. It was a Mass like any other, but as this Mass ended, the priest surprised me by inviting those in need to come forward for the anointing of the sick. But he didn't actually use the word "sick." Not exactly.

"Come forward," the celebrant said, "for whatever kind of healing you need."

As I had done previously on similar occasions, I intended to slip out quietly. Indeed, I had already turned to do so. But people had expected this service. To my surprise, as I moved toward the doors I found myself hemmed in by wheelchairs. Briefly, I recalled another occasion when I'd been similarly "trapped." Then, I'd sat in the pew and let people climb over me. I thought of doing that now, but it wasn't possible. The slightest maneuvering caused pain to shoot from my shoulder like a laser.

"I'm caught," I said to myself. And I considered the consolation: "I *do* need healing."

The priest that day was a Jesuit. "Concentrate on the pain," Father Boly instructed.

"Well," I thought to myself with some irony, "I can't help but do that!"

Father Boly, meanwhile, continued the instruction. "When you come forward," he intoned, "whisper what you ask healing for."

Still caught in the flow, I walked forward with the crowd. "My shoulder," I whispered.

When anointed with oil, I experienced nothing. (Of course, I hadn't *expected* anything.)

In the end, in fact, it took seven days for me to admit that it had even happened. The pain that had shot through my shoulder immediately after the Mass – and in all those weeks preceding that Mass – had burned with such ferocity that I kept bracing myself for its return.

Even though the pain did *not* return, I still had trouble believing I was healed.

But I was. Months have elapsed. I'm pain free even now. Totally pain free.

Usually I see my doctor only once a year. But I had been invited into an experimental group dealing with women's health, and a physician's report was required. So, a few months later, I returned to my doctor.

"How's your shoulder?" the doctor asked.

I told him the whole story.

"Your doctor couldn't heal you," he said gently, "so God did."

Meanwhile, I've changed my mind about Extreme Unction – with apologies to God. Fortunately, God has a terrific sense of humor.

And so, you see, God definitely does hear prayers for healing. I now walk up for the anointing of the sick every time I get an opportunity.

Healing from the inner pain of a loved one lost is no different from physical healing. It's certainly no less important. Through the anointing of the sick, God can effect either.

No matter what faith you are, no matter Who your God is, it is imperative to ask for healing – particularly when you have nowhere else to turn. I can even imagine God musing on this subject from time to time, in a state of puzzlement. "*Why don't they ask?*" I imagine God saying. "*I didn't make them stupid. Somehow, those human creatures never turned out like I thought they would!*"

God wants our prayers, especially when we're hurting.

Accept that Mourning is Painful.

The pain we feel when we lose a loved one is, in itself, a tribute to the love we shared together. It's precisely because my sister and I loved each other so much, for example, that my sense of loss has been so keen.

Contemplate Your Own Mortality.

Death is a reality for you and me, as well as for those we mourn. Coming to terms with the finiteness of life on earth can help us attain inner tranquility.

I love life, and enjoy my work. But I know an end is coming. And, in a way, I look forward to death. I'll meet and embrace my mother, father, and Eileen again. How much we'll have to talk about and share! I think of them daily. I'm certain they're interested in me, and help me from heaven. Some day, there's going to be a great meeting Up There.

Know That the Pain Will Eventually Take on Some Perspective.

I'll never stop loving and missing my lost loved ones. But, when we've grieved well – and thoroughly – we'll come to terms with having lost them.

The pain of loss with my mother and father was even more keen than with Eileen. Gradually, over the years, that pain has eased. They're full of joy in heaven, suffer no more pain or worry. They wouldn't want to come back, and I try to rejoice with them. I talk to them, often, and ask their help when the going gets rough.

Today, I can talk about my parents easily. Eventually the same will be true of Eileen.

Trust Your Heart in Getting Your Needs Met.

Some days the pain will be too much to bear. Do we need a friend? Remember the pal who said "If you need anything, just call"? Perhaps it's time to pick up the phone.

Other days, we may simply need to remember. Or have a good cry. Let your heart lead you.

Summer before last I could not, absolutely could not, enjoy a vacation in any location that Eileen and I had shared together. But last summer I knew I could manage.

Because I was marking more than 60 years in Religious life, my Good Shepherd Sisters allowed me to celebrate in whatever way I wanted. I have often longed to see the art and treasures of Italy. Because our headquarters are in Rome, that would become my destination and the place where I could hang my hat, so to speak. Though Eileen and I had made one brief trip to Rome, and had then stayed at our Generalate, it no longer hurt too much to go. Now I could remember her there in a special way, but without the searing pain of loss. I was ready for a good time, a time to enjoy. And I did, I really did.

The loss of a loved one affects each of us differently. Perhaps it's when we reach out to help others that we most clearly sense the loved one, invisible but nearby.

Hundreds of volunteer opportunities surround us. If only to help ourselves, we might join our local St. Vincent de Paul Society chapter, or tutor at our neighborhood school, or phone the Red Cross to find what we might contribute. In reaching out to the poor, the disabled, and the suffering, we touch the face of God. And when we touch God's face, we experience healing.

SUMMARY

Death hurts. For those of us left behind, going on can be a challenge indeed. But it's no tribute to the loved ones we've lost to stop living. No, we must go on. With God's help, it can be done.

Highlights

- Denial, anger, deep sadness – all are elements of grief and must be worked through.
- Regrets after the death of a loved one are not uncommon. It's all right to have them, and all right to let them go.
- Praying for healing from grief is always an option. It's no different than praying for physical healing, which many of us do often.

Discussion

1. Have you lost a loved one? Whom did you lose? How is life different now?

2. Write down some treasured memories. Why were those times so special?

3. How might we move on – when we're ready? Is helping ourselves through helping others an option for us? What might we do to make this happen? List a few local charities where your services might be needed, and where your skills might be put to good use. When will you call to offer your services?

TWENTY

Live Well, Age Well

Antony the Great, founder of Christian monasticism, was born in Egypt about 251, and he was baptized when he was 20 years old. He was a rich young man. But after his parents died, Antony gave away his money and went to live in the desert.

Life alone in the desert, of course, might sound like a wonderful, fanciful escape: a pleasant, solitary life alone with no worries while we sit beneath a date palm.

But I've visited the Egyptian desert, traveled through it. And I can tell you that I never want to see it again. The heat is absolutely beyond description. It was so hot there that none in my tour group wanted food or water, nor would we have eaten had our guide not warned us over and over, "You *must* drink water. You *must* eat. If you don't, you'll go to the hospital for a very long time."

So living in the desert is no picnic. But when the awful persecutions of Christians during the first centuries began, this was enough to drive countless men and women into the wilds. Others fled to the deserts to escape the licentiousness of the cities. And many of these exiles became disciples of Antony. He, in turn, taught them how to live in the desert – with and for God alone. Today, in fact, Antony is known as "The Star Father of Monks." Never ordained a priest, he lived a hard, difficult life using only God as his personal compass. And he stayed alive for 105 years.

Occasionally persons who come to me for counseling discuss their fear of aging: loss of income, wrinkles, and the resultant physical disabilities – and these are people who are by no means chronologically "old." Indeed, the men and women I'm talking about range from their 20s through their 40s. As I listen, I sometimes wonder whether aging is the real problem for these people.

A couple of nights ago, for example, a woman of about 49 said, "If I could have anything I wanted, I'd choose breast implants and a tummy tuck." Her thought is to look good, of course. In some measure all of us want that. But isn't *who we are* more important than *how we look?*.

That's why somebody like Antony, The Star Father of the Monks, is a good role model for us as we age. Not only because he lived for a long time, but because he lived well.

Father Robert, who founded the Trappists, offers yet another fine role model. Born of a noble family in 1027, he joined the Benedictines in the diocese of Troyes, France. As a young man he was chosen prior, then elected abbot of a different monastery in France. Apparently not fond of his position as superior, he resigned. A few years later he was again chosen prior, then another abbey elected him abbot.

Eventually, though, Father Robert left that post also, this time founding a reformed monastery in a swampy plain in Burgundy, later called Citcaux. Father Robert never intended to found a new Order, but in time his reformed monastery led to the establishment of the Cistercian Order, popularly known today as the Trappists. And despite the demanding lifestyle of the Trappists – it is considered the most rigorous of religious Orders – Father Robert lived to be 83. One hundred years later, he was canonized.

And most of us, including non-Catholics, have heard of St. Teresa of Avila who founded the Discalced Carmelites. Affectionate and lively and gifted with good judgment, Teresa was respected and loved by many – and hated by many more. When necessary she stood up to authorities, both civil and ecclesiastical. Always, Teresa held her head high before adversity.

"Beware," she warned one provincial superior when he strongly disapproved of her ideas, "of fighting against the Holy Spirit."

To a troubled young nephew she wrote that God's mercy is great. Then, she took charge of the child he'd fathered before marriage as well as the young man's seven-year old sister, bringing them into the Convent for child-care until they might be old enough to fend for themselves in the world. "We ought always," she remarked to her Sisters, "have a child of this age among us."

Still, in spite of her generous nature, Teresa's efforts to reform the sixteenth century Carmelites met with stiff resistance.

Her case was even remanded to the Inquisition. Nevertheless, by her sixth decade of life, Teresa had established 15 contemplative reformed Carmelite convents – in a time when travel meant riding on a mule or in a jolting carriage over unreliable roads.

Always amid her struggles, she kept good humor. And, perhaps because of her deep faith, she was no worrier. On one occasion, for example, she and another nun took possession of a house that had been occupied by some students who'd reportedly had "little or no regard for cleanliness." The women's goal was to turn the rundown abode into a convent. But the house was large and eerie. That night, the other nun got nervous. As they lay on piles of straw for the night, Teresa asked the Sister what was bothering her.

"I was wondering," the woman said, "if I died here now – what would you do with a corpse?"

"I'll think about that when it happens, Sister," the unflappable Teresa replied. "Now go to sleep."

When she died at age 65, Teresa was still founding convents, though she was no more popular than she'd been as a younger woman. But that never stopped her from speaking her mind.

Consider, too, Benedetta Rossello. Born into a poor family in Italy in 1811, Rosello landed a job with a wealthy family in Savona at age 19. Though she wanted to join a convent, Benedetta could not; she didn't have money for a dowry. So she continued working, sending the money she earned home, hoping better opportunities would come her way.

As it turned out, the bishop of Savona was looking to establish an Order to benefit the girls and women of the region. And when Benedetta volunteered to help him do this, the bishop gladly accepted her offer. Immediately Benedetta, two cousins, and a fourth young woman took up residence in a shabby house in Savona. They began calling themselves Daughters of our Lady of Mercy.

The young women's possessions were few: a couple of sticks of furniture, some straw mattresses, a sack of potatoes, a crucifix, a statue of Our Lady, and about one dollar in currency. Their plan was to educate poor girls and, later on, open hostels, schools, and hospitals.

By 1840, Benedetta, now Sister Josepha, had been elected the new Order's Superior. She was 29 years old. And she had only just begun.

Before long, her Order had permeated northern Italy – but not without difficulty. Sometimes the Sisters met with clerical opposition, and they had money problems. Nevertheless, Savona's Bishop had always wanted rescue-homes for young women who had "strayed," and with his blessing, Mother Josepha succeeded in establishing several.

Indeed, it is said that whenever Mother Josepha had $5 on hand, she started a new project. One such venture was the House of Clerics; its goal was developing priestly vocations. By 1875, Mother Josepha's Sisters were founding missions in Buenos Aires, Argentina. Mother Josepha, meanwhile, kept her form by working out regularly – with brooms and dust cloths – sweeping floors, polishing tables, and doing laundry.

By age 64, though, she had developed heart trouble. She was not able to be up and about. Did she quit? No way. Though she could only oversee work, not do it, Josepha continued as Superior for the next five years until her death. "Cling to Jesus," she repeated over and over again to her community. "There are God, the soul, eternity; the rest is nothing."

St. Josepha Rossello died in 1880 and was canonized in 1949.

Yet another fine example of living well and aging well is the foundress of my own Order, the Good Shepherd. Born in France in 1796, just as the French Revolution was in its dying throes, Rose Virginie Pelletier enjoyed a happy childhood. As she approached adolescence, however, all that changed.

Orphaned in her teenage years, Rose Virginie joined the Sisters of Our Lady of Charity of the Refuge in Tours, 1814 – an Order founded in France, 1641, by St. John Eudes to help girls and women recover from moral distress and exploitation. The early years of Sister Mary Euphrasia's life were spent in direct ministry to girls and women. She was elected superior at the age of 29. Under her spiritual leadership, the community and apostolate took on new life. At the bishop's invitation, Sister Euphrasia founded a house in Angers in 1829. It was called "Good Shepherd" in memory of a previous house which had done similar work.

In 1831, Sister Euphrasia formed a contemplative community for girls and women under her direction who desired to consecrate themselves to God.

Longing that the whole world benefit from the saving work of St. John Eudes, she saw the need for a centralized government so Sisters could be sent to all peoples. After many difficulties, the Generalate was approved in 1835. Thus, the Church established Angers and Convents dependent on it as a congregation distinct from the Order of Our Lady of Charity. The new congregation was called "Our Lady of Charity of the Good Shepherd of Angers." Mother Euphrasia – who never intended to found a new Order – became Superior-General of the apostolic and contemplative branches of the Good Shepherd Sisters.

Mother Euphrasia had a clear view of her mission: that women and girls acquire grace and beauty in God's sight. She was appalled by slavery: God's children sold in markets like animals. Good Shepherd Sisters were poor, but Mother Euphrasia implored them to save every penny to ransom slave children, educate, and set them free.

A Presentation Sister often shared dinner at the Good Shepherd. Each time she noticed that Mother Euphrasia filled the first plate, and sent it for a poor person who might knock on the Convent door.

In France, up to 1850, children under 16 were imprisoned with adults for minor offenses such as homelessness, theft and lies. Then laws changed, and adolescents could go to new structures like farms or "correctional" schools. They might come to the Good Shepherd in large groups, from 30 to 100. Mother Euphrasia welcomed them with new dresses (to get out of prison garb), blazing fireplaces, and hot dinners. Where did she get the money? Nobody quite knew.

The Congregation became world-wide and was divided into provinces, 1855, by the Church. Difficulties continued. Money and food were always in short supply. Not to mention the ongoing problems of travel – by horse, coach and sailing ship.

Sometimes coach drivers had emptied too many glasses of wine before they set out; occasionally, carriages broke down or tumbled over. In Europe, Mother Euphrasia might be on the road continuously for four months at a time.

Meantime her Sisters were reporting that their cupboards were empty, that they had no food.

"What shall we do?" they asked her.

"Only have faith," she answered, "and God will provide."

At age 71 she celebrated her Golden Jubilee, joyfully marking 50 years as a Good Shepherd Sister. But Mother Euphrasia's health began to fail.

Though she continued to keep ahead of her competent secretaries by generating voluminous correspondence, the day came when she had to face facts: she was losing ground to illness.

Characteristically, Mother Euphrasia embraced God's will.

"It's time," she directed matter-of-factly, "to notify all the Houses."

"That's been done," she was told.

Mother Euphrasia was pleased. "Good," she said. And then she named, one by one, each of the 110 Houses scattered over five continents. As she neared death, Superiors arrived from various convents and she greeted each by name, giving a special message to each convent and its Sisters. On the last day of her life, she reached out in love to her missions in distant lands in similar fashion. And then it was time for farewells.

"Goodbye," Mother Euphrasia said to those gathered around her. "I commend you all to God." When she breathed her last, she was 72 years old. She was canonized in 1940.

A common myth holds that memory skills decrease with age. Not necessarily. It's true that as we age, neurons die off. Thus, the brain must establish new pathways among its myriad switches. In doing so, however, it may become even more sophisticated than before. That's right, our brains might actually get *better* with age; but we do have to use them.

We learn from Father Antony, St. Teresa of Avila, St. Euphrasia, and all the others — most of whom, by the way, are now saints — that a purposeful, active life and an open, active mind are the best exercises for aging well. And it doesn't hurt to do work that we love while enjoying lives of moderation and purpose. The saints certainly did!

SUMMARY

The Catholic Church is rich with stories of people who made great contributions all through life, including their twilight years. There's no reason for us to be somebody different later in life than we were during our younger years. But to be productive in old age, we must keep productive all through life. To this end, an active mind and body and a lifestyle of moderation continue to be the best antidotes for fighting aging's big challenges.

Highlights

- Many people who fear aging really are dissatisfied with other aspects of their lives.

- Physiologically speaking, aging need not affect our minds or the quality of our lives.

- *How we live* has an irrevocable effect on *how we age.*

Discussion

1. What kind of person do you want to be in the twilight years of your life?

2. Given your present lifestyle, is this goal realistic?

3. What kind of life adjustments can you make now to possibly improve your quality of life in old age? How will you keep active mentally? Physically?

4. Are you doing what you love? How might you further enrich your quality of life *now*?

TWENTY-ONE

Failure Can Be a Beginning

To the people of his time, Jesus might well have *seemed* a failure. Indeed, even by today's standards, especially to movers and shakers who hold out for glitzy goals, Jesus may *appear* to be a failure still.

How can we say this?

Jesus never wrote a book. Jesus never sat on the panel of a national television talk show. Jesus never preached on the radio.

- Jesus never earned big wages.
- Jesus was an itinerant preacher who walked from town to town on his own two feet.
- Jesus never attracted the huge following of some televangelists.
- Of the 12 persons committed to Jesus, one betrayed him – and the rest ran away, leaving him on his own before those who had come to arrest him.
- Jesus was given the death penalty.
- Jesus died on a cross, a criminal's death.

But Jesus Also Rose Again. Triumphant. To Live Forever.

In doing so, the message he left us is clear: Hand in hand with the divine Jesus, we can turn even our most apparent failures into successes.

Each of us has already failed one way or another. Even saints have failed in their day. St. Benedict Joseph Labre, for instance, certainly looked like a failure.

He applied to and tried out several Religious orders, but was either turned down or dropped out of each one. In time, he became a kind of street person, wandering from one religious shrine to the next. St. Benedict was not especially clean, nor was he well-fed.

But when he collapsed and died on the streets of Rome one day, the everyday people knew a treasure had been lost.

"Our saint," they cried out, weeping, "is dead."

And they were right. The miserable-looking wayfarer was indeed a Saint. His steadfast devotion, prayer, and belief, even in the face of adversity, made him a role model and an inspiration to everyone he ever met – and to us, too, when we read his story in the chronicles of the saints.

Failure is an event, that's all. And it is, moreover, an event that can be turned around in a variety of ways.

Of all forms of failure, getting fired is probably the worst. It results in loss of self-esteem, money, and that job by which, so often, we define ourselves. Because it's done *to us*, it leaves us feeling out of control. Sadly, today, many persons *do* lose their jobs.

My client Dave was fired. Not a person to sit around and weep, however, Dave busied himself finding other work. And when he noted an international art contest in the *London Review of Books*, Dave entered the contest. He had, after all, secretly dreamed of being an artist most of his life; he just never thought he could measure up.

But now Dave had nothing to lose. And though more than 26,000 entries poured in, Dave took first place. Today, Dave is self-employed as an artist, earning many times the money paid by his former job, and winning prestige and acclaim. *"You're fired!"* provided Dave the opportunity of a lifetime.

Being fired isn't the only time we might feel we've failed. Sometimes it's our health that lets us down. Jean had to relinquish her very good job because of cancer surgery and chemotherapy. In her early 40s when her health broke down, Jean felt very much alone. She had, in the past, always tithed 10% of her income to the Church and charitable endeavors. Should she continue?

Would her money run out? Jean decided to tithe on faith. And she never regretted her decision.

When Jean regained health enough to work full time, she never had to hunt for work. One by one, companies called on *her* for advice and consultation. Before she knew it, Jean had become a free-lance consultant with a salary at least as good as that which she had to forfeit because of illness.

Dave and Jean are entrepeneurs who succeeded. *But entrepeneurs can also fail.* Can they take failure more easily than the rest of us? No. Failure is particularly tough for the entrepreneur because the person often feels he or she has only him- or herself to blame.

But entrepeneurs do have an advantage over the rest of us. Most have a dream. And because it is *their* dream, they believe in it. Often, of course, they're right. If they stick with a good idea long enough, most entrepreneurs can win.

Scott Adams, creator of the comic strip *Dilbert*, is a case in point.

Adams sketches Dilbert and his cartoon friends in a simple, almost childish style. Indeed, a newspaper feature syndicate, which rejected his strip five years ago, suggested that he take art lessons. In fact, Adams had applied to a cartooning school at age 11, but was rejected as too young. Finally, during his college years, he enrolled in a drawing course. But he got the lowest grade in the class.

In time, *Dilbert* grew out of Adams' doodles, scribbles he made during mind-numbing meetings at his place of employment, PacBell.

Colleagues loved these clever creations. But when Adams submitted his *Dilbert* strips to *The New Yorker* and *Playboy*, both rejected them.

Then he submitted to the major newspaper syndicates. Everybody turned him down except United Media.

United Media has not been disappointed with *Dilbert's* performance. Says Janine Hallisey, United Media vice-president of marketing, "We haven't seen a strip move this quickly since the early years of *Garfield*." Currently, *Dilbert* is featured in 260 newspapers, and its syndication grows at the rate of 10% a month. More recently, *Dilbert* became the first major strip available on the Internet.

What if Scott Adams had become so discouraged by all the rejections that he quit?

In the face of failure, Scott Adams stuck it out.

We need to remember that:

- Failure is just a word.
- Failure is not a condemnation of our character.
- Failure doesn't mean we have a fatal flaw.
- Failure is a road-block everybody encounters at some point.
- Failure is not the end of life.
- Failure can turn into a dawn of hope.

Then too, in some cases, the failures we face may not be our own. Sometimes we're faced with the consequences that result when others have failed us. Certainly, this was Betty's predicament.

Unfair as it may seem, at such times we still need to hang in there. That's what Betty did, and it made all the difference.

Betty was only four when her mother divorced, and put her in a Catholic orphanage. The little girl loved the life there. She made friends, started school, and felt happy. Then, suddenly, her mother turned up with a new husband. Abruptly she informed Betty that she was taking her "home."

Betty wept bitterly. The orphanage had become her real home. But Betty's mother insisted. Betty was seven now, and her mother had a husband; like it or not, the child was going "home."

Betty's stepfather, though, was a brutal man. He beat the little girl frequently. Since Betty's mother never intervened, Betty's life became a nightmare. Periodically she ran away, but the police always found her. Bruises and beatings showed.

No matter. The police always took Betty back home. This was the 1940s, and because she was a minor, they said, her word against her stepfather's would not stand up in court. Finally, when an aunt turned 18, she went to court with Betty and testified to the savage beatings she had watched Betty endure. At age 16, Betty was court-committed to the Good Shepherd School in Seattle as a neglected and dependent child.

Betty arrived with a BB slug in her neck; her mother had shot her with a BB gun because Betty had picked a flower.

Betty was incredibly beautiful. I'll never forget her big blue eyes, blond curly hair, unusually fair skin – or her gratitude. Betty was overwhelmingly grateful to have a safe, peaceful place to live.

Very bright, she graduated from school at age 17. Since the court had committed her until she was 18 or had graduated from high school, she consequently returned home. Her mother assured her and us that this time life would be different.

Of course, Betty's stepfather beat her up again. And Betty ran away again. This time, back to the Good Shepherd School. Principal at the time, I arranged for Betty to take business courses from Seattle University for the next two years.

Meantime, Betty's mother became terminally ill. A Catholic, she had not practiced any religion for years. Betty longed for her mother to have a happy death. And so Betty prayed rosary after rosary.

Betty's faith won out over defeat. Her mother returned to her Catholic faith and did have a peaceful death.

Betty, meanwhile, was only 19 and would not hear of leaving our Good Shepherd haven. But it was time for Betty to make it on her own. We had given her the tools; now Betty had to build a life of her own. To help her along, we filled two suitcases with new clothes, bought her a ticket to Spokane, and rented her an apartment there. We even drove her to the train.

Though the young woman did not want to strike out on her own, Betty wasn't about to embrace failure, either. She immediately set about finding a job. In three days, Betty received 15 job offers. She took the best one. Eventually, Betty became private secretary to a vice-president at Boeing.

Betty could have tumbled into self-defeating behavior. Instead she turned a troubled youth around and enjoyed a good life.

Another illustration of somebody who built something out of almost nothing is Rose. When Rose was separated from her husband, she was too confused to decide immediately whether to continue the marriage. Previously, Rose had lived as a full-time homemaker, and now she felt discouraged, helpless, and off-balance.

But Rose was not without resources. Rose is tall, slender, and good-looking. Her dress is always exquisite. She learned how to dress, she once told me, because of her height. Always, she stood head and shoulders over other students, young women, and her friends. Because of her self-consciousness, Rose took time to discover how to make herself attractive.

In group therapy with me, Rose offered to provide several sessions to the women in her therapy group illustrating how to dress appropriately on slender budgets. "Women," she said, "can dress to advantage, even on a Kmart budget."

Obviously, Rose knew what she was talking about. Months after therapy concluded, I saw Rose's photo on the front page of one of Seattle's daily papers. She had obtained a substantial grant to teach low-income women how to maintain excellent appearances for job interviews. Rose looked competent and fulfilled.

Over the years I have watched not just adults, but thousands of teenagers turn their lives around as well. Betty was by no means the only one. Indeed, I'd have to say the most spectacular turnaround by far that I ever witnessed occurred in more recent years with a young woman named Marvel.

Here, Marvel Davis tells her own story:

I lived pretty much on the streets of Detroit from about age 14. This was back in the early '60s. Drugs hadn't taken over the streets yet, so fortunately I didn't get into them. We didn't do much of anything in those days except hang out.

My father worked days, and my mother nights. But mother would scarcely be gone for work when dad would head out on the town. My brother, sister, and I were alone virtually every night, and school time always seemed to come much too early each morning. Eventually, we just dropped out.

One day a truant officer picked me up. That's when the Juvenile Court sent me to the Good Shepherd school in Detroit, a residential treatment center for teenage girls in need of school and protection, as well as for kids in conflict with the law.

I needed education for sure, but I needed love more. I needed somebody who'd listen and care.

As a Baptist, I knew nothing about nuns – no more, in fact, than I knew then about Baptists. But the Good Shepherd Sisters who ran the place loved us kids. They didn't throw tax dollars at us. We got nothing ritzy. But they cared.

Getting adjusted took time: three meals a day, hot cooked food, clean clothes, clean sheets, regular hours, school. These weren't things I was used to. The routine certainly turned my old life around like a windmill. For the first few months I was dizzy as a whirlybird.

I could have left in a year, but I had nothing to go to. Nobody to go to. And, all the while, I kept thinking, deep down inside: Someday I'm going to help kids like me.

One nun in particular helped me: Sister Marie. She was a psychologist. We talked a lot. She told me they had a small book of rules for child-care written by the Foundress of the Good Shepherd Order, Sister Euphrasia. "So that's why she aways tries to look strict," I thought, "and that's why it never works!" Silently, I told myself: "That's how I'm going to take care of kids someday."

I graduated from the Good Shepherd school and got two diplomas: high school graduation and a state license in cosmetology. I settled down in a trailer. At age 19 I applied for my first foster-child: a boy whom I later adopted. Then a little girl, whom my husband and I adopted. It was a beginning.

Now 26 years later, Jim and I have provided a home for 170 children placed with us by the juvenile courts; usually we have about five at a time. Right now we have five boys: Four are teenagers.

About 15 years ago Jim and I decided to give priority to teens, maybe because we felt they needed it most. Both of us definitely love kids.

Let me tell you about one of them, Dick. We've had Dick for a while. He's brain-damaged. Before coming to live with us, Dick could attend school only in self-contained learning classrooms. After staying with us for a while, though, Dick began to feel stifled in learning-disabled spaces. He insisted on – and got into – regular classes.

Today Dick works extremely hard, spending three times the usual hours of study to keep up. And he needs lots of help. But his attitude has zoomed up to the stars, so teachers and kids are always happy to give him time and a helping hand. Dick is in his senior year now, and he recently made the rowing team for the second time. It's so thrilling for Jim and me to watch him grow.

Through the years, we have had many other experiences that left us feeling as fulfilled as our experience with Dick. There was, for instance, the time tragedy struck a local family: Their house burned down. For a while, three of the 15 children lived with us. We were happy to do what we could.

Some days are anything but smooth, of course. The first couple of times a child of ours was expelled from school, I was at a loss for what to do. But then Jim and I came up with a very practical solution: Any child who is expelled sits at the kitchen table during the hours he or she would be in school and works at his or her studies. Just as in school, the youth raises a hand to go to the bathroom. There's no talking, no TV, no radio. Just silence and schoolwork. These days, our teenagers are very seldom expelled from school.

Detention posed a problem for a time, too. But not anymore. If one is kept late because of misbehavior, getting home becomes that child's problem. We live in Rockwood, a suburb of Detroit, and the school is four miles away. Four miles is not an unreasonable walk for a healthy teenager. Besides, a child in our home can always phone home to obtain a ride – at a cost of 22 cents a mile. Should a child have detention for several nights, a bike can be ridden to and from school. (We don't have many detentions either.)

All our foster-children go to church Sunday mornings. It's not a rule, but they usually agree on the church themselves and take off, all together. Some children come to us with no religion, some have never seen the inside of a church, and a few have attended regularly. But each Sunday, regardless of background, they all go to church. Every single one of them. They always have.

I myself talk to God all the time, ask God what to do, how best to deal with a troubled child, how to gift a lonesome, frightened child with love. I depend on God. And I have that little book St. Euphrasia wrote, the book that states her ideas about caring for troubled children. This wise woman's advice can best be summed up in one word: love.

It helps to know I'm not alone, not in anything. Sometimes problems seem insurmountable, and might well be except for my husband's help. He's great, especially with teenage boys. He takes them fishing and sets a good example in helping around the house.

In fact, many of our foster-children are now young men and women themselves, living throughout the United States. We frequently receive letters, phone calls, visits, telegrams, and flowers. Our home is piled with thank-you notes. And just last month the county commissioners threw a party for me over at juvenile court.

All because God, many years ago, made a home for a lonely teenager. With love.

Marvel never gave up, never lost hope.

She turned her life around, and has turned the lives of countless others around ever since.

Failure need never be the end. Failure can become a wonderful beginning. Both failure and success, with God's help, need only be a state of mind. The choice, always, is ours: What will it be?

SUMMARY

Sometimes life's biggest opportunities knock at our door dressed in failure's attire. At such times, only hope, faith in ourselves, and faith in God can help us turn things around. We also need to evaluate what contribution we might make to our own cause and then incorporate the necessary changes. Just because we've failed in one area of life doesn't mean we must fail ourselves. And just because somebody else has failed us doesn't mean that God has failed us too.

Highlights

- Failure is an event, that's all.
- By today's – and even ancient – standards, not even Jesus was a rip-roaring success.
- When we fail, we must take stock and work ever harder at success.
- God and prayer can sustain us in tough times. And God and prayer can help us succeed.

Discussion

1. Is fighting discouragement just as important as fighting failure? Why or why not?

2. Why is failure "just a word"?

3. Why is Jesus a questionable success story by today's – and yesterday's – standards? Do you agree with this assessment? How does society define success? How do you define success? Can you reconcile the two in your own life? How?

4. Have you ever failed? When? How did you handle it?

5. What makes the people featured in this chapter true successes? Would you like to be like any of these people? If so, in what ways?